T0145616

Hints for Lovers

Hints for Lovers

Arnold Haultain

MINT EDITIONS

Hints for Lovers was first published in 1909.

This edition published by Mint Editions 2020.

ISBN 9781513266541 | E-ISBN 9781513266985

Published by Mint Editions®

MINT
EDITIONS
MintEditionBooks.com

Publishing Director: Jennifer Newens
Project Manager: Gabrielle Maudiere
Design & Production: Rachel Lopez Metzger
Typesetting: Westchester Publishing Services

Table of Contents

Plea: Confession and Avoidance

"... aphorism are seldom couched in such terms, that they should be taken as they sound precisely, or according to the widest extent of signification; but do commonly need exposition, and admit exception: otherwise frequently they would not only clash with reason and experience, but interfere, thwart, and supplant one another."

—Issac Barrow

"The very essence of an aphorism is that slight exaggeration which makes it more biting whilst less rigidly accurate."

—Leslie Stephen

Chapter I

On Girls

"A Pearl, A Girl."

—Browning

There are of course, girls and girls; yet at heart they are pretty much alike. In age, naturally, they differ wildly. But this is a thorny subject. Suffice it to say that all men love all girls-the maid of sweet sixteen equally with the maid of untold age.

There is something exasperatingly something-or-otherish about girls. And they know it—which makes them more something-or-otherish still:—there is no other word for it.

A girl is a complicated thing. It is made up of clothes, smiles, a pompadour, things of which space and prudence forbid the enumeration here. These things by themselves do not constitute a girl which is obvious; nor is any one girl without these things which is not too obvious. Where the things end and the girl begins many men have tried to find out.

Many girls would like to be men—except on occasions. At least so they say, but perhaps this is just a part of their something-or-otherishness. Why they should want to be men, men cannot conceive. Men pale before them, grow hot and cold before them, run before them (and after them), swear by them (and at them), and a bit of a chit of a thing in short skirts and lisle-thread stockings will twist able-bodied males round her little finger.

It is an open secret that girls are fonder of men than they are of one another—which is very lucky for the men.

Girls differ; and the same girl is different at different times. When she is by herself, she is one thing. When she is with other girls she is another thing. When she is with a lot of men, she is a third sort of thing. When she is with *a* man. . . But this baffled even Agur the son of Jakeh.

As a rule, a man prefers a girl by herself. This is natural. And yet is said that you cannot have too much of a good thing. If this were true, a bevy of girls would be the height of happiness. Yet some men would sooner face the bulls of Bashan.

Some foolish men—probably poets—have sought for and asserted the existence of the ideal girl. This is sheer nonsense: there is no such thing. And if there were, she could not compare with the real girl, the girl of flesh and blood—which (as some one ought to have said) are excellent things in woman.

Other men, equally foolish, have regarded girls as playthings. I wish these men had tried to play with them. They would have found that they were playing with fire and brimstone. Yet the veriest spit-fire can be wondrous sweet.

Sweet? Yes. On the whole a girl is the sweetest thing known or knowable. On the whole of this terrestrial sphere Nature has produced nothing more adorable than the high-spirited high-bred girl.—Of this she is quite aware—to our cost (I speak as a man). The consequence is, her price has gone up, and man has to pay high and pay all sorts of things—ices, sweets, champagne, drives, church-goings, and sometimes spot-cash.

Men are always wishing they knew all about girls. It is a precious good thing that they don't.—Not that this is in any way disparaging to the girls. The fact is

A girl is an infinite puzzle, and it is this puzzle, that, among other things, tickles the men, and rouses their curiosity.

What a man doesn't know about a girl would fill a Saratoga trunk; what her does know about her would go into her work-box.

THE LITTLEST GIRL IS A little women. No boy knows this—and precious few grown up men. Thus

Many a grown up man plays with a girl, then finds himself in love with her. As to the girl—

Always the girl knows whether the play is leading: she probably chooses the game.

VERY LATE IN LIFE DOES a man learn the truth (and significance) of that ancient proverb that Kissing goes by Favour. For

The masculine mind is the slave of Law and Justice:

Aphrodite never heard of Law or Justice: she was born at sea. That is to say,

Few are the men who at some time in their lives have not wondered at the vagaries of girlish complaisance: the foolish, the ne'er-do-well, the bully, the careless, the cruel,—it is to these often that a girls' caress is given. And,

Curiously enough, that is, curiously enough as it seems to purblind law-loving man,—should the favored one be openly convicted, that alters not one whit his statue with the girl; for,

A girl, having given her heart, never recalls it not wholly: she may regret; she never recoils. In other words,

To the man of her own free lawless choice a girl is always loyal; to subsequent and subordinate attachments she is dutiful. So,

Even the renegade, if loved by a girl, will be upheld by that girl through thick and thin—secretly, it may be, for often the girl, nevertheless devotedly, and only under compulsion will he listen to the detractor: he may desert her, or, if he sticks to her, he may beat her; no matter: he holds her heart in the hollow of his hand. But, But,

Few things mystify poor law-abiding man than this, that the central, the profoundest, the most portentous puzzle of the universe— the weal of woe of two high-aspiring, much-enduring, youthful human souls, should be the sport of what seems to him the veriest and merest chance.

THE UNCONSCIOUS SEARCH OF SWEET sixteen is for (in mathematical language which will not sophisticate her) the integral of love.—Yet

In the short years between sixteen and twenty a girl's love will undergo rapid and startling developments.

A GIRL WITH LOTS OF brothers has more chances of matrimony than a girl with none: she knows more of men; especially of their weaknesses and idiosyncrasies. And

To know the weaknesses and idiosyncrasies of men is perhaps a wife's chief task; unless it be to put up with them.

OFTEN ENOUGH THE FRECKLED AND fringrant girl wins over the professional beauty.

SOMETIMES GROWN-UP GIRLS ARE JUST as shy as little ones—and for the same reasons because there is no one who knows how to play with them.

Girls often play with love as if it were one of the amusements of life; but a day comes when love proves itself the most sensuous thing on earth. And

A girl is quick to discover the kind of love that is required of her. As a rule

Many a girl who has been sore put to it to prove herself whole-hearted. For of course,

Always every suitor expects whole heartedness. And this every girl instinctively knows. Indeed,

Is not a half-hearted love, or a half-hearted acceptress of love, a contradiction in terms?

A CERTAIN MEASURE OF THE sophisticated or unsophistication of a youthful damsel may be found in her manner of receiving the attentions of a stranger in a station different from her own.

Young women, themselves but rarely unsophisticated, view with a certain pitying sort of curiosity unsophisticatedness in men. And

A young man's unsophisticatedeness it is a great delight to a woman to eradicate. Yet

A girl regards with complex emotions the man who has blossomed under the genial warmth of her rays; the flattery to own powers is counterbalanced by the evidence of lack of power in him.

A GIRL THINKS SHE DETECTS flippancy in seriousness. A woman thinks she detects seriousness in flippancy.

WHAT WOULD BE CONDUCT DECIDEDLY risqué in a city miss, is often innocent playfulness in a country maid.

BETWEEN THE AGES OF SIXTEEN and eighteen, girls play with love as if it were a doll; very soon after twenty they discover it is a dynamo. This is why

An early and clandestine engagement often works more havoc than happiness. For

Either, one of the parties to the concealed compact receives or pays attention which perturb the other; or, a subsequent and acknowledged lover looks askance at the previous entanglement. Since even if

A clandestine engagement (as is usually the case) is merely a flirtation with the emoluments which accompany a promise to marry, those

　　　　　　　　　　　　　　　ARNOLD HAULTAIN

emoluments are not nice things for a subsequent and avowed lover, whether masculine or feminine, to think upon. Lastly,

A laxity with regard to the claims of courtship is apt to breed a laxity with regard to the claims of wedlock. In short,

Flirtations, like clandestine engagements, are an affront to love. Accordingly

To the engagement-ring should be as attached as much importance as to the wedding-ring. Indeed,

A difficult and a delicate path it is that a girl has to tread through life—and often enough a dangerous. Yet with extraordinary deftness she treads it. She must win her a mate, yet has to pretend that the mate wins her. She makes believe to be captured, yet has herself to be intent on the chase. To be wooed and wedded is the law of her being, yet not for one moment dares she to exhibit too great an alacrity to obey that law; for she knows instinctively that an easy victory prognosticates a fickle victor. Is she abundantly endowed with the very attributes that make for wife-and-mother-hood, a strong and swaying passion and an affection unbounded, she must hold them in leash with exemplary patience; for, alas! Are they given the rein for a single passing moment, instead of being accounted unto her for righteousness, they work her ruin. She must win her one man, and she must win him for life; but she cannot pick or choose, for she must wait to be asked.

If she make test of many admirers, she is described as a flirt; if, conscientious and demure, she await her fate, a desirable fate is by no means assured.

In truth it seems that too often a girl must dissemble—hateful as dissemblance in men. T'is a hard road indeed that a girl has to travel. To win her a fellow-farer for life, she must go out of her way to accommodate so many travelers: and this one is lured by this, and that one by that, and another by something unnoticed by the throng. But, an she dissembles one iota too much, her fellow-farers look askance, and he who eventually joins her for good upbraids her for that by which she won.

DISSEMBLANCE IS INDEED AT ONCE the boon and the bane of a girl: without it, she thinks to be overlooked (often enough a preposterous assumption); with it, she is looked upon too much. And always,

Always a girl has to pretend that never did she descend to dissemblance.—Which, nevertheless, is sometimes absolutely true, for

Just now and then there happens that miracle of miracles, where their flames up in the man, and their flames up in the maid, in both at once, unaided and unlooked-for, that divine and supra-mundane spark which smolders lambent in every youthful breast: when maid and man take mutual fire at touch of hands and look of eyes,—fire lit at that vestal altar which knows no source and burns for aye.

Chapter II

ON MEN

"Duskolon esti to thremma anthropus."

—PLATO

For man, the over-grown boy, life has commonly two, and only two, sides: work, and play. Happy he who has for a helpmate one who possesses the faculty of increasing a zeal for the first and of adding a zest to the second. Wherein, O woman, thou mayest happily find the two-fold secret of thy life-work. For

Man is a greedy animal: he wants all or nothing. And fortunately for him,

Women tacitly extol man's greed: they will not be shared any more than they will share.

There is something canine in the masculine nature: like a dog over a bone, it snarls at the very approach of a rival.

IT IS CURIOUS, BUT IT is true, that proud man becomes prouder (and—more curious still—at the same time humbler) when weak woman gives him something—a look a smile, a locket, her hair, a kiss, herself.

THE GREATER A MAN'S FAITH in himself, the greater his mistress hers in him. And perhaps, the greater his mistress her faith in a man, the greater his in himself. For

A woman's faith in a man works wonders.

A MAN TO WHOM A woman cannot look up, she cannot love. Yet,

It is marvelous how a woman contrives to find something to look up to in a man.

MANY MEN FORGET THE ARTISTIC tendency of the feminine temperament, a tendency which shows itself in many ways—their love of pretty things, of pretty ways, and of pretty words. From which three alone we may deduce the rule that

When with the woman he admires and whose admiration he seeks, a man cannot be too careful of his dress, his speech, and his manners.

A BELIEVER IN WOMAN IS a believer in Good. And vice versa, and mutatis mutandis.

MAN'S STANDARD OF VALUE OF a woman is usually determined by the scale of his own emotions. That is to say,

The pedestal upon which a man places a woman (a man always puts a woman upon a pedestal) is a pedestal erected solely by the effect upon himself of her charms.

A MAN MAY BOAST HIMSELF invincible by men; never by woman.

THE LADY-KILLER IS ALWAYS AN object of attraction to ladies, even to those whom he makes no attempt to slay.

IT MAY PERHAPS BE A thing as unreasonable as certainly it is indisputable, that however much wild oats a man may himself sow, he invariably entertains a very peculiar objection to any woman near or dear to him entering upon this particular branch of agriculture.

HE IS A FOOL WHO does not bear himself before his lady-love as a prince among men.

SOME MEN ARE SO GALLANT that they will never be outdone by the woman who encourages them. But it often leads to strange embarrassments and entanglements.

FEW THINGS TERRIFY A MAN more than the knowledge of a woman's ability to make her emotions—when, if ever, he arrives at it.

THAT IS A VERY SILLY man who thing she can play one woman off against another. For

In matters of emotional finesse the masculine instance is nowhere: it is blinded, befogged, befooled at every turn.

Heaven help the man who is dragged into a quarrel between two wrathful ladies!

THREE THINGS THERE BE—NAY, FOUR—WHICH man can never be sure, how a greatsoever his acumen, his astuteness, or his zeal: a woman; a race horse; a patent; and the money-market. They defy both faith and fate; they should be the recreations not the resources of life; and he is a fool who stakes more than a portion of his substance on any one of them.

WHAT A PALTRY THING, AFTER all, is man, man uncomplemented by woman! Left to himself, he stagnates; linked with a woman, he rises—or sinks. A gentle touch stimulates him, a confiding heart makes of him a new creature. Under the rays of feminine sympathy, he expands who else would remain inert. Fame may allure him, friends encourage him, fortune cause him a momentary smile, but only woman makes him; and fame, friends, fortune, all are naught if there be not at his side a sharer of his weal. A man will strive for fortune, strip himself for friends, scour the earth for fame; but were there no woman in the world to be won, not one of these things would he do.

Chapter III

On Women

From woman, who e're she be, there seems to emanate a potency ineffable to man,—impalpable, invisible, divine. It lies not in beauty or grace, not even in manner or mein; and it requires neither wiles nor artifice. It is not the growth of long and intimate acquaintance, for often it acts spontaneously and at once; and neither the woman who possesses it nor the man who succumbs to it can give it a name. For to say that it consists in the effluence or influence of personality or temperament, of affinity or passion, of sympathy or charm, is to say nothing save that we know not what it is. All unknown to herself, it wraps its owner round with airs the which to breathe uplifts the spirit, and yet, may be, perturbs the heart, of man. Even its effects are recondite and obscure. It allures; but how it allures now man shall tell. It impels; but to what, does not appear. It rouses all manner of hopes, stirs sleeping ambition, and desires and aspirations unappeasable; but for what purport or to what end, none stays to inquire. It incites; sometimes it enthralls. It innervates; it exhaults. Under its spell, reason is flung to the winds, and matters of great mundane moment are trivial and of no account: for it bewilders the wit and snatches the judgment of sane and rational men. It is most powerful in youth; it is most powerful upon youth; yet some retain it till far on in years, and no age but feels its sway:—a veiled and mysterious force; sometimes daemonical, often divine: at once the delight and the despair of man. After all,

The man who declares he understands women, declares his folly. For,

If woman were not such a mystery, she would not be such an attraction. For again,

What is known is ignored. (But woman need have no cause for apprehension.) Besides,

Men may be classified; women never. This is why

Generalizing in the case of women is useless; since

Woman is a species of which every woman is a variety. And every man must make up his mind to this, that

Every woman is a study in herself. However,

If women were comprehensible to men, men and women would be friends, not lovers (But the race is safe). The simple fact is that

Womanliness is the supreme attraction, in however fair or however frail a personality it is embodied. And

The sacred function of all womanhood is to kindle in man the divine spark by means of the mystic flame that burns ever in the vestal breast.

Every true woman's orbit is determined by two forces: Love and Duty. Which is another way of saying that

Women, like the lark, are true to the kindred points of heaven and home. But,

It is only when the two foci are coincident and identical that her orbit becomes the perfect circle and her home becomes her heaven.

A woman's heart is an unfathomable ocean: nothing ever filled it; no one ever plumbed it. At the surface are glancing waves, or flying spume, or, it may be, raging billows; beneath are silent depths invisible to man. A thousand streams flow into it in vain. Towards varying coast-lines it bears itself variously; here, placid and content; there, dashing furious. But none ever stamped his marked upon its brim, and always it remains the refluent, reluctant sea. Of it man knows only the waves that break or ripple at his feet. It betrays no secrets; it asks not to be understood. Storm and calm but stir or still its surface, and what things it hides forever engulfed no one may learn. Subtle, yet mighty; an eternal, and entrancing, mystery to man.

A man's heart is the enclosing shore; measurable, impressionable, definite, and overt; thinking to house that sea, shaping it, over looking it, and staying and governing its tides. Yet changed by it, crumbling before it, yielding to it: at once its guardian and its slave. Yet perhaps

The placidest of seas is that which is wholly land-locked.

Women, apparently, were made for men; men for themselves. Certainly

Men seem to carry out this design of Nature, that they should be ministered to by women.

A WOMAN ASKS A WOMAN questions in order to discover something. She asks a man questions in order to discover the man.

HE LAST THING THAT A woman will risk is her personal appearance. Which is saying a good deal, for
   A woman will risk an interview at an unseasonable hour, but not in an unseasonable frock.

NEVER, NEVER TAKE A WOMAN *au pied de la letter*.

WOMEN'S RIGHTS ARE: TO BE loved.

WOMEN'S DUTIES ARE: TO LOVE.

THERE IS ALWAYS SOMETHING SOVEREIGN and monarchial about a woman: like a queen's, her wishes are her commands. And
   In matrimony, woman's sovereignty is not abdicated. By no means; it is only transformed from an absolute into a constitutional monarch : she acts then by and with the advice of her First Lord. This is the ideal State.

WOMAN'S TRUE FUNCTION, AS A citizen, in this world is: to spur men on to high and noble action. And this, quite unconsciously, she does.
   Woman's true function, as a woman, in the world is: to evoke man's most fervid emotions, and at the same time to keep them at their highest level. And this she also does—perhaps not quite so unconsciously.

THEY ERR WHO CALL WOMEN illogical. Feminine logic is inexorable. But it proceeds *per saltum*. It is man who has laboriously to reason step by step.

THE MOST WAYWARD WOMAN CRAVES control: To let a woman have her own way is interpreted by her as indifference. And
   The surest way to fail to please a woman is to let her do what she pleases.

WOMAN IS BORN TO ACTING as the sparks fly upward. And
   What a woman really is, nobody knows, least of all herself. To see a woman as she really is, one must see her with her babe. For

ARNOLD HAULTAIN

It is curious, but it is true, that not even before the passionate and accepted lover to whom she has utterly devoted herself can a woman bare her heart as can she to her babe. Perhaps we may go so far as to say that

Motherhood always partially eclipses wife-hood:

When the child comes, the man stands aside. For

It is not within the capability of man to evoke or to develop the totality of woman. There are feminine potentialities he is powerless to awake. There is a portion of womanliness always hidden from him. To her babe alone she opens the innermost recesses of her soul. For him she wears no masks, affect no accent, plays no part. Even her features take on a different and unique expression before the offspring of her womb. Never is she more womanly, never so strong, never so quite, never so self-contained, never so completely herself, and never so beautify when bending over her helpless infant son. And naturally: for say what one will,

Motherhood is the goal of womanhood. And

Howsoever she comes by it, a woman's burthen is always to her "That Holy Thing". So

No one knows what a woman is like till she is a mother. In other words

Motherhood reveals womanhood. And, be it remembered,

There be childless women—both spinsters and wives—who could mother mankind in their bosoms. Such women wield great influence. For

Many a mere man there is has owed his all to a motherly woman.

Nor speech, not restore, nor expression of feature, nor all combined, will ever reveal the real feelings of a woman. To unbosom herself is impossible to woman. Do not expect it, for

Definite and accurate utterance is not given to woman.

The chief business of woman is: first, to get married; second, to get others married.

It is difficult to say which have played the greater havoc among men: the women with too much conscience, or the woman with none.

When a woman repulses, beware. When a woman beckons, be warier.

Woman are always prepared for emergencies.

With woman, tact and jealousy rarely go hand in hand; tact and spite never.

The only instance in which a woman's tact is apt to be at fault is in detraction of a woman whom she regards as her rival;

The instance in which a woman's tact is seen as its best is in deploying the men who she knows are rivals for her hand. And usually

When a woman has more than one admirer, she not only deploys them, but tries to make them advance en echelon. For

Few things disconcert a woman more than a multiple and simultaneous attack delivered front a front. But

The way in which a woman will maneuver her attackers is marvelous.

They say a woman cannot argue. Hear her explain an indiscretion!

An independent woman is a contradiction in terms. For Woman's chief want is to feel that she is wanted. Therefore it is that

With women, cruelty is more easily borne than coldness. Indeed, It is astonishing how much downright cruelty a woman will stand from the man she loves or has loved. On the other hand,

Melancholy also attracts women. Naturally,

Women are made to soothe, to pity, to comfort, to delight. Therefore it is that

To see a strong man in a weak woman's arms is a sight which should arouse—not our laughter, but our envy. So it does.

Let not the simpleton think a woman will sympathize with his simplicity:

No woman is a simpleton.

What women admire is a subtle combination of forcefulness and gentleness.

If a woman has to choose between forcefulness and gentleness, always she will sacrifice the latter. And

It is astonishing to what lengths forcefulness can go without endangering a woman's admiration. If it sweeps her off her feet. . . well,

In nothing does a woman so clearly exhibit the inherent femininity of her nature as in the delight with which, at the bottom of her heart, she recalls moments when she has been swept off her feet. She may sigh over them; but

Generally, a woman's sighs are by no means those of remorse. A woman never brings pure reason to bear upon her actions; she acts by sentiment and she judges her acts by sentiment. This is why

Even when a woman has deceived and betrayed, she does not regard herself culpable. Always, she says to herself, she was driven to it, and therefore she is blameless. Accordingly

A penitent woman is rare:

Even when a man, with his so-called superior reason, thinks he has proved her wrong, at the bottom of her heart she knows herself right.

MANY HAVE BEEN THE DISCUSSIONS as to woman's most powerful weapon. The simple fact is, she is armed cap a pie. Indeed, Every woman is a sort of feminine Proteus, not only in the myriad shapes she assumes, but also in her amenability to nothing but superior force. Women form, perhaps, where men are concerned, the single exception to the rule that in union there is strength. One woman often enough is irrepressible; two (be the second her own mother) break the charm an association of women is the feeblest of forces.

ALL WOMEN ARE RIVALS. AND this they never forget. Consequently

Mistrust a truce between hostile ladies.

AMONGST WOMEN, MODESTY IS OF infinitely more potent influence than is ability. Yet

To a woman's modesty ability is a wonderfully enhancing setting. And

Modesty is the most complex and the most varied of emotions. Perhaps

When modesty and frailty go hand in hand, there is no more delectable combination known to men; and Aphrodite has not the subtle charm of a Cynthia. Perhaps this is why such

A wondrous halo of romance hangs about the name of a Heloise, of a Marguerite, of a Marianna Alcoforado; of a Concetta of Afragola; of a Catalina; of Robert le Diable's Helena, of Isolde; of Lucia of Bologna, the enchantress of Ottaviano; of Francesca; of Guenevere; of the sweet seventeen-year old novice of Andouillets, Margarita, the *fille* who was "rosy as the morn"; of the Beguine who nursed Captain Shandy; of the *fille de chamber* who walked along the Quai de Conti with Yorick; of

Ameilia Viviani, the inspirer of Shelly's most ecstatic lyric; of Dryden's masque-loving Lucretia. For, after all,

Is the star any the less starry to the rapt star-gazer when he finds it to be a tremulous planet?

Cynthia may have blushed in heaven; bit did the blush make her any less lovely to the Latmian?

Only in the clear and unclouded pool is the star undimmed embosomed.

THEY SAY A WOMAN IS capricious. But the consistency of woman's capriciousness is only exceeded by the capriciousness of man's consistency.

Man calls woman capricious simply because he is too stupid to comprehend the laws by which she is swayed. Woman does not call man capricious.—The inference is obvious.

TO WOMEN THE PROFOUNDEST MYSTERIES of the universe give place to two things: a lover, and a baby.—But perhaps these are the profoundest mysteries of the universe.

HOW MANY WOMEN THERE BE who, deeming themselves fitted to be the consorts of kings, yet comport themselves dutifully as the wives of wastrels! And indeed,

Given beauty, cleverness, and grace, there is no position to which a woman could not aspire; for

Being Woman, she is ex officio Queen.

SPEAK TO A WOMAN DISPARAGINGLY of her sex,—she is up in arms.

Speak to her disparagingly of a member of her sex,—well, she will not be up in arms. The reason for her bellicosity in the former case is the fact that

A woman always interprets abstract disparagement of her sex personally. And she is perfectly right.

IT IS NOT ONLY THE woman who cannot be accounted quite as stainless as the stars that sometimes trade on their charms.

WHEN A STRONG-SOULED WOMAN WHOLLY and unreservedly loves, her love will go to lengths passing the comprehension of man. For

Women prefer an despot to a dependent.

It is marvelous to what a pitch of demureness features by nature that the most coquettish can be set.

(A Man's features are often a clue to his character; a woman's rarely.) So it comes about that

The owner of a seraphic face is often owner of a temper satanic. Nevertheless,

Often enough a spice of diablerie in a woman at once enhances all her charms.

It is indeed fortunate for the men that so many women are unaware of the power of their charms.

A woman would much rather you lied to her concerning herself than that you told her something unpleasant to hear.

Some women seem to be envious of some men's familiarity with immorality.

It is by woman that a woman will be first suspected; and it is by a woman she will be last forgiven. The last thing a woman will ask you for is: your esteem. And yet

Cast a slur upon a woman's character and you are considered indiscreet. Cast a slur upon a woman's personal appearance, and you are considered culpable.

Fashion is a woman's sole law. And

The surest evidence of strong-mindedness in woman is to fly in the fact of fashion.

Ridicule is woman's keenest weapon; it is the poisoned arrow in her quiver. Well is it for the men that she never, or so rarely, has recourse to it.

A woman is quick to discern the quality of the admiration bestowed upon her.

No one, not even herself, knows what a woman will do next.— Doubtless this is trite. But it is true as trite. Yet men rarely find it out till late in life—and forget it as soon as found out.

A woman can say more in a sigh than a man can say in a sermon.

Nothing piques a woman so much as indifference to her favors. Indifference to her undiscovered passion she quite otherwise regards.

The woman knows the male heart probably better than does it itself. She knows above all things, that to hold that heart she must never wholly satisfy it. And many—and multiform—and marvelous—are the ruses by which she accomplishes that end. And yet,

Women there are who firmly believe that, were they to try, they could enthrall any man beyond possibility of extrication. And so perhaps they could; but the achievement would require as much unscrupulousness as it would seductiveness.

The seductive and unscrupulous woman is hatred of women.

Under the gaze of a group of men whom she knows that her brilliancy dazzles, a woman, like the snow-clad hearth, sparkles: Under the gaze of a man by whom she knows she is passionately desired, like the same earth under the lordly sun, she melts.

All women think they can cozen men: few women think they can cozen women.

The women who perturb men most are those who combine too effectively adorableness with desirableness.

As in nature, so in humanity, flight on the part of the lady is not always symbol of unwillingness of pursuit. On the other hand

Feminine audacity by no means betokens feminine immodesty.

Feminine obduracy is invincible by man. Luckily, it is rare.

Men call women variable: did she not vary, men would tire. This, women instinctively know.

Women rightly dislike and disgust variability in men. For

Women like best to be liked: to lead gives them but paltry and temporary pleasure. (Though this they do not always instinctively know; or, if they do, they conceal their knowledge.) And

Variability is incompatible with leadership.

How delicately a loving woman reproves! How defiantly an unloving!

How many lonely women—married and unmarried—the world contains, only these lonely women know.

The feminine métier par excellence is: to allure. And

The subtle and elaborate means by which women will devise to intensify the lure, passes the comprehension o f men. Yet

In all ages, to make herself attractive was as right and proper for the woman as to make himself feared was for the man. Besides,

With women the art of attracting has long since become second nature.

Women are quick to recognize a rake. For

A rake always rouses curiosity, never aversion.

A worsted woman always, either silently or volubly, calls down a curse upon her successful rival.—And 't is a curse that too often fails.

Many women handicap other women; and they handicap them in multifarious ways. Probably the one most frequently used is lavishness of favors.

The woman who is lavish of favors is hated of her stricter sisters. But, before these, what an air of bravado she wears!

As a rule, women are far better readers of character than are men. A woman will often startle a man by her penetrating insight into character. And

Many a man has been put on his guard by female institution.

The fragilest woman will be ill content with suppressed embraces. And

The ablest-bodied woman loves being petted. Even

A prude is a shy coquette.

The man who judges of a woman by her letters is a fool.—Her gesture will contain more matter than her journal. Besides,

The woman who could punctuate could reason.

The debut of a younger sister evokes mixed emotions.

The prayer—uttered or unexpressed—of many an undowered young woman is, May a moneyed man fall in love with me!

And she is not always over-careful to add, And may I fall in love with that moneyed man!

IF THE "NEW WOMAN" TURNS out to be a fitter companion for men than the old, no man will complain of her novelty. Yet

Men regard the advent of the New Woman rather askance. Why? Because

To judge from certain feminine utterances, the New Woman seems more inclined to aim at rivalry than at companionship with man.— However, there need be no fears as to the result, since

Such is the mysterious potency of womanhood, that, whether new or old, woman will always lead man captive. Besides

As every new variety of fashion in dress seems becoming to women, so, it is probable, every variety of fashion in manners will become them also. But probably

The phrase the "New Woman" is not unlike the phrase the "New Chemistry": the materials are the same; what is new is the nomenclature.

A WOMAN'S PECCADILLOES ARE GENERALLY worse than a man's. At all events they are more reprobated.

ABASHMENT INTENSIFIES A WOMAN'S LOVE for him so making her abashed. And

There is a shame that is sweeter than joy. (As

There is a fear more tremulous than delight.) For

Mastery is a woman's standard of man. And There is an element of the freest and frankest savagery in the most refined and spiritual of women. (How otherwise

Can any one explain the extraordinary fable of Selene and Pan?— And man?

—But that man was ever a savage. It may be added that

The defenselessness of woman is a conventional fiction: she can avert an attack by a look; she can terminate a siege by a taunt.

SOLOMON HAS OBJURGATED THE INVINCIBLY garrulous woman. The invincibly taciturn woman is so rare as to have escaped objurgation. Yet she too is a terror to men.

EVERY WOMAN IS SUSPICIOUS AND jealous of any woman that opens a man's eyes; even though she knows that

Never was there a woman who could and would deliberately wholly enlighten a man.

And, yet, marvelous and curious amongst things curious and marvelous, will but a woman fling artifice to the winds, and look and act and say as great Nature prompts,—wildly, willfully, wantonly,—that woman will captivate as no feminine wiles will ever captivate.

IF THE MAN WERE WORTH it, many a woman would dispense with the marriage ceremony. For

Ah! Love—love—love,—given love, what else is needed? (Unfortunately

Love can never be sure of itself—much less of anything else. Accordingly

The marriage contract is a device on the part of the community to provide for the preservation of the home: it makes the parties promise fidelity.) But

Precious few are the men who are worth the risking. Unfortunately,

More women succumb to strength of will than to strength of character.

Neither, in general, are women overcurious to enquire whether the strength of character.

Neither, in general, are women over curious to enquire whether the strength of the masculine will makes for good or for evil.

So long as the masculine will overmaster the feminine, the feminine mind is satisfied. Of course there are exceptions, but as a rule,

Women—whether young or old, married or single, strong-minded or weak—are never happier than when they can depend on a man. Accordingly,

The lover or the husband who is weaker than, and depends upon, the woman, will some day rue his weakness and dependence. And yet,

To see a strong male at her feet—that is exquisite to the woman. So exquisite that

It is with difficulty that a woman refrains from exhibiting a man's servitude to others. On the other hand,

There is an element of intimidation in a resplendent woman. And of this she is aware.—Hence perhaps her power.

A WOMAN WILL ATTAIN HER ends by adroit finesse, where a man would blunder into open hostility. And

It is well that man should blind his eyes to feminine wiles, since,

Always a woman kindly pretends oblivion of masculine blunders.

The woman whose tastes and refinements are above her station, is in pitiable plight: she is too fastidious to espouse the men who would marry her; the men she would marry she rarely meets. For, The only thing that, to love, is insupportable is vulgarity. Since

Love, romantic love, the efflorescence and bloom of life, is besmirched unless tenderly touched.

To generalize passes the wit of woman; but in penetration she is preternatural.

What fascinates a woman is the man who unwittingly attracts her against her will. But such a man rouses a combination of emotions comprehensible only by women.

A woman's answer to an insuperable argument is: a look. And a most cogent answer it is. Indeed,

Speech is a woman's least effective weapon; rarely if ever does she resort to it:

In the affairs of life, as in the affairs of love, where men be concerned, it is upon her personality that she relies, not upon her speech whether written or uttered.

Her personal appearance is to a woman, what his personal honor is to a man: it must be immaculate; constant with the fashion of the hour; and strictly in accordance with her or his status in society. Accordingly,

Dress and demeanor—these form the code of feminine ethics. Even

Deception on the part of a woman is merely diplomacy;

Women deceive only be cause man is too blind to see. That is to say,

Since man in past ages has never allowed woman either freedom of action or frankness of speech, it is not to be expected of her that she should be all at once an adept in their use.—To her credit be it said that,

Generally a woman deceives only n order to arouse or to retain the admiration of man. For example,

Many a woman has surreptitiously made love to the man—and few are the men who have detected it.

Why this woman fascinates all who come within the sphere of their influence, and that women, does not, no earthly sage will ever know. As well ask what makes one man a Napoleon, another a poltroon. So, too,

It is impossible for a woman to say 'I will be loved,' as it is for a man to say 'I will be obeyed.'—Perhaps

Love and Power are divine miracles.

(At the risk of treading on delicate ground, ground off which I shall be hooted by the modern woman, I venture to say that)

The idea that a woman is the property of the man of her choice, rail as it as the woman may, has not yet been ousted from the feminine mind—and heart. Indeed,

So firmly implanted in the feminine breast is the idea of the ownership of her by the man, that it is to the man who assumes and exercises ownership that she clings. This is why

A woman easily changes her allegiance; since,

Allegiance, to a woman, means loyalty to the man who assumes and exercises ownership over her:

Let a man who a fractional part of a second evince the shadow of a doubt of his proprietorship—at once he undermines a woman's allegiance. Consequently,

It is folly for men to express amazement at the ease with which a woman will transfer herself and her affections.

A woman will transfer herself bodily over and over again, but only because the previous owner lightly esteemed, or weakly maintained, his ownership. As a matter of fact

In pristine days woman was, naturally and necessarily, the property, the chattel, of the man: marriage was not then a matrimonial syndicate of two: marriage meant that a woman sought a provider, a supporter, a defender; the man a mate for his delight, his comfort, and his solace, a keeper op is cave or hut, a mother and nurse for his heirs. And provision, support, and defense, being, in pristine days, matters of strength, prowess, or cunning, naturally and necessarily pristine man gained him and kept him a mate by strength, prowess, or cunning; he regarded that mate as his by right of force, not as a partner in a compact. And

The most complicated of modern communities has no whit altered the relationship of man to mate, conceal though it may the origin and history of marriage. Finally,

No woman at the bottom of her heart has any objection to being owned. Indeed (though no woman would say it, a man may),

Every woman at the bottom of her heart delights to be owned, and tacitly and secretly seeks the man who she thinks will glory in that ownership and keep his property safe—not only from material harms, but from temptations to changes of ownership. In which last little fact lies a curious truth.

Women like to be defended against themselves. In this little matter men and women differ: That any other man should dare for one instant to covet or alienate that most precious of his possessions, his mate,—nothing rouses to a higher pitch man's unappeasable wrath than this;

Against the man so daring, a woman's wrath is never roused: rather she regards him as one having discernment, and his daring is a commendable compliment to herself. In fine, and in short,

Allegiance, to a man, on the part of a woman, means, in her eyes, loyalty to him who properly exercises the right of ownership. In simple truth,

A woman gives herself to a man: to the man who proves himself worthy the gift, she is true.

And this is why women, all women, even the New ones, love being petted and admired and made much of all their lives: this but proves the possession of the gift to be appreciated. Besides,

The male is the dominant animal—not necessarily in his cave or his hut,—by no means, but in the stress and struggle of life; and women tacitly (though never openly) look up to and admire this dominance, even when exercised over themselves; since This, in turn, proves the masterfulness, the worth, of the man; albeit sometimes they rebel against it if carried to far. At least,

Unless a man continues to exhibit his appreciation of the gift by word as well as by deed, the woman is apt to imagine that that appreciation is on the wane.

ARNOLD HAULTAIN

Chapter IV

On Love

"Amore che muove il sole e l'altre stelle."

—Dante

The beginning, middle, and end of love—is a sigh.

All things point to the infinite; and love more than all things else.

Complex as is the character of love, here are two things which love always does: always it

"Refines the thoughts
And heart enlarges;"

—Milton

and,
    Love dyes all things a cerulean hue. (What a pity it is not a fast color!)

Love is the most antimonial of emotions: it worships, yet it will not stop at sacrilege; it will build about its object a temple of adoration, then desecrate the fane; it will give all, yet ruthlessly seize everything; it delights in pleasing, yet it sometimes wittingly wounds; its ineffable tenderness often merges into an inclemency extraordinary;—symbol of universal duality, it is at once demonical and angelic.

Nothing stands still in this world, not even love: it must grow or it withers. And, perhaps,
    That is the strongest love which surmounts the greatest number of obstacles.

Love to some is an intoxicant; to others an ailment. To all it is a necessity.

As is one's character, so is one's love. And
Perhaps the deepest love is the quietest.

Love is as implacable as it is un-appeasable. Nay more,
Love is merciless: as merciless to its votary as to its victim: For
Love would slay rather than surrender; would for-swear rather than forgo.

Some loves, like some fevers, render the patient immune—at all events to that particular kind of contagion.
Many lovers are vaccinated in early youth.

Only love can comprehend and reciprocate love. This is why,
If, of two sensitive human souls, the one loves passionately and the other not at all, the other is unwittingly blind and deaf to love's clamors and claims: the one may ardently urge; the other but passively yields:—
Only the famished understand the pangs of the hungered.
Of a great and reciprocated love there is one and only one sign: the expression of the eyes. Who that has seen it was ever deceived by its counterfeit?
Did ever the same love-light shine in the same eyes twice?
The light of love in the eyes may take on a thousand forms: exultant jubilation, a trustful happiness; infinite appeasement, or promises untold; an adoration supreme, or a complex oblation; tenderness ineffable, or heroic resolves; implicit faith; unquestioning confidence; abounding pity; unabashed desire. . .
He who shall count the stars of heaven, shall enumerate the radiances of love.

There is no Art of Loving; though, as Ovid says, love must be guided by art. Yet,
If love did not come by chance, it would never come at all.

To each of us himself is the centre of the visible universe. But when love comes it alters this Ptolemaic theory. Yet,

It is a significant fact that love, which, more than any other thing in this world, is the great bringer-together of hearts, begins its mysterious work as a separator and puter-at-a-distance. For

When love first dawns in the breast of youth, it throws about its object a sacred aureole, which awes at the same time that it inspires the faithful worshipper.

CAN ONLY TWO WALK ABREAST in the path of love? How many try to widen that strait and narrow way!

LOVE RAISES EVERYTHING TO A higher plane; but nothing higher than the man or woman who is loved.

Is there anything about which love does not shed a halo? Indeed,

Love is a sort of transfiguration. And when on the mount, we can very truly say, "It is good for us to be here".

If there is any sublunary thing equal in value to the true love of a faithful woman, it has not yet entered into the heart of man to conceive.

TRUE LOVE MAKES ALL THINGS loveable,—except perhaps the chaperon.

Was there ever man or woman yet who was not bettered by a true love?

True love is ever diffident and fearful of its own venturesomeness. But this not every woman understands.

Too often the Phantasm of love and not the Verity wins the day. Women who seek a real lover should beware the overbold one.

TO MERGE THE THEE AND the ME into one—that is ever the attempt of love. It is impossible. Yet, perhaps

They are happiest who can longest disbelieve in the impossibility of this amatorial fusion; for it may be that such

Incredulity is favorable to romance.

LOVE IS NOT EXACTLY A sacrifice; it is an exchange. The lover, indeed, gives his heart; he expects another in return.

LOVE IS LIKE LIFE: NO apparatus can manufacture it; kill it, and nothing in the heavens above or in the earth beneath or in the waters under the earth will resuscitate it.

How many a forlorn human wight has tried to resuscitate love!

To such heights does love exalt the lover that he or she will live for days in the remembered delights of a look, a word, a gesture. But

One thing is impossible to love: love cannot create love; the intensest and most fervent love is powerless to evoke a scintillation of love.

Love may worship, it may adore, it may transfigure, it may exalt the object of its devotion to the skies; but it cannot cause that object to emit one ray of love in return.

Hate may be concealed; love never.

The greater the imaginative altitude of love, the lower the boiling point. But

Love cannot always be kept at high pressure.

The young think love is the winning-post of life, the old know it is a turn in the course. Nevertheless, it is a fateful turn.

In love, the imagination plays a very large part. And this may be variously interpreted. Thus,

By man, love is regarded as a sort of sacred religion; by woman, as her every-day morality. The former is the more exhilarating; but the latter is more serviceable. Indeed,

Love and religion are very near akin: both inspire, and both elevate. And

If faith, hope, and charity are the basis of religion, there never was such as religion as love. And

Love is the only religion in which there have been no heretics. Why? Because woman are at once its object and its priesthood.

Love, art, and religion are but different phases of the same emotion: awe, reverence, worship, and sacrifice in the presence of the supreme ideal.

Love knows no creed. Nay more,

Love acknowledges no deity but itself and accepts no sanctions but its own: it is autonomous. And yet—

And yet, love sometimes feels constrained to offer a liturgical acquiescence to the rubric of Reason. In short,

Between the prelatical domination of Reason and the recusant Protestantism of Love there has ever been strife. Or, in plain language, There are two codes of ethics: one that of the romantic heart; the other that of the practical head. Who shall assimilate them?

ARNOLD HAULTAIN

The heart, in its profoundest depths, feels that something is due to Reason; and Reason, in its highest flights, feels that something is due to the heart.

Is there a divine duplicity in the human soul? And yet, after all,

All love seeks is: love. Yet love little knows that

In seeking love, love enters on an endless search. Since

Love is an endless effort to realize the Ideal. For

Love always beckons over insurmountable barriers to uninhabitable realms; promises insupportable possibilities; lures to an unimaginable goal. Yet

Love has a myriad counterfeits. And

Men and women interpret the word differently. Even

Different women interpret the word love differently. Thus,

To one woman, love is as the rising of the sun: it shines but once in her whole life-day; it floods everything with its light; it brightens the world; it dazzles her.

To another woman, love is as the rising of a star: a fresh one may appear every hour of her life, and nor she nor her world is one whit affected by its rays. Indeed, one would hardly err if he said that

Many a woman really does not know whether she is "in love" or not. She is sought—that she perceives; but which of her seekers is worthiest, which most zealous, which merely takes her fancy, and which appeals to her heart—on these matters she meditates long—to the exasperation, of course, of the individual seeker. Accordingly,

Men, carried away by their own passionate impulse, detest calculation of the part of women:

Since HE stakes his all on impulse in the matter of love, says man, why should woman stay to consider? Foolish man! he forgets that

A woman always weighs a man's declaration of love—and legitimately— and naturally; perhaps legitimately because naturally; for, once again,

What a woman stays to consider in the matter of love is, not the potency of the impulse of the moment, but the permanent efficacy of the emotion. Therefore it is that

Woman unwittingly obeys great Nature's laws.

MANY IMAGINE THAT LOVE IS a thing like a chemical element: with a fixed symbol and a rigid atomic equivalent. And so it may be; but, like the philosopher's stone, hitherto it has defied detection in its elemental form. The fact is probably that

Love may be compared to a substance that is never found free, and which not only combines in all sorts of relationships with all sorts of substances, but also, like many another chemical body, takes on the most varied forms, not only in these relationships, but also under varying pressures and temperatures.—Or perhaps it would be better to say that

Love may be compared to a musical note: to the unthinking it is a simple sound; to the more experienced it is know to consist of endless and complicated harmonical vibrations; harmonizing with some, and making discord with other, notes by regular but unknown laws; differing according to the timbre of the emitter; reverberating under certain conditions; lost to the ear in others; and only responding to resonators vibrating synchronously with itself. Lastly,

There is a whole gamut of love.—Changing that simile, we may say that

Love is not like the sun: a unit, and practically the same wherever seen; it is like light: all-pervading, universally diffused, and reflected and refracted and absorbed in varying degrees and varying manners by various objects. And

Than a great and pure love, can anyone point to anything on earth greater and more purifying?

The lesser luminary perturbs the tide of human passion; the greater light draws it upward—none the less veritably because in tinted formless vapor. This is symbolical of love.

It is the nascent thing that evokes the keenest emotions: the bud—the babe—dawn—and the first beginnings of love. So Love, like sunlight, wears its most tender tints at dawn.

It still remains a mystery that, out of a townful of folk, two particular hearts should worry themselves into early graves because this one cannot get that other. Yet

It is almost enough to destroy one's faith in the uniqueness of love to see from how narrow a circle of acquaintances men and women choose their spouses. Were Plato's two half-souls separated by the diameter of the globe—that were lamentable.

The man often argues that esteem will grow into passion. The woman knows that the argument is utterly fallacious. Yet Unless passion is guarded by esteem,—as the calyx ensheaths the corolla, the former is prone to wither.

In youthful love, as in the enfolded bud, esteem and passion—like calyx and corolla-—seem one and identical;

It is only the full-blown flower that displays its constituent parts.

Would that love could remain ever in bud!

TO SOME LOVE COMES LIKE a flash; to others as the burning of tinder.

In all, when real love is kindled, it devours all that is combustible. But

All love, like all fire, needs, not only ventilation but replenishing:

Unless the primal spark is nourished, it will not glow;

Stifle love, and it dies down. So

Even the love of a married pair, unless it retains something of the romance of courtship, is apt to go out.

LOVE TAKES NO THOUGH OF surroundings: an empty compartment is as good as a coppice. Give it privacy, it is satisfied.

IN LOVE, WE WOULD MUCH rather give than take. Yet, if the giving is one-sided, there is trouble. And

Love brooks no half measures. Again,

Trust a woman to calculate the breaking-strain of her lover's heart. But she will never let him off with less than the maximum stress.

WHEN LOVE IS DEAD, IT is perhaps best soonest buried.

IN ASTRONOMY, TO DETERMINE THE motions of three bodies mutually attractive is admittedly difficult. It is easy compared with the same problem in love.

A MAN'S WORK AND A woman's love, though to each the sum-total of life, are often things wholly and totally dissociated.

Man, the egoist, thinks that if the woman loves him, by consequence she will love his work. It may be, but usually, non sequitur; for

Few are the women who can understand a man's work:

For thousands of years man has worked in the hunting-field, in the market-place in the camp; for an equal length of time woman has worked by the cradle, by the hearth. Accordingly,

Man has two sides to his nature, woman but one:

Man wears one aspect when facing the world; he wears quite another aspect when facing women;

At their work, men are rigid, frigid, austere, sever, peremptory, tyrannical, downright;

With women, . . . Humph!—Wherefore,

O strenuous and high-aspiring man, in thy work, seek not from woman's love what woman's love cannot give; but set thy face 90 as a flint. Bethink thee of the fate of Anthony. For

Man's chief business in the world is: Work.

Woman's chief business in the world is; Love.

Man's love (perhaps just because it is his play-thing, not his business) is more finely tempered than is woman's, and takes on a finer edge. For this very reason it is the more easily turned, and is the less useful.—It is the pocket-knife, not the lancet, that is oftener called into requisition. Also,

Man's love is usually a highly ephemeral affair.

With a man, love is like hunger or thirst: he makes a great fuss over it; he forgets when it is appeased. Yet

When "passion's trance" is overpast, it is fortunate if affection takes its place. So too,

In love it is the man who protests; and

That man is fortunate, who, after marriage, has not some dubious reflections as to whether he has protested over-much. For

In love, it is the man, generally, who makes a fool of himself.

LOVE (LIKE MURDER) WILL OUT. But

Jill keeps her secret better than Jack. For

A woman generally controls love: a man is controlled by it. And Jill's very power of making-believe to be "fancy free" exasperates Jack.

IT IS A PURELY FEMININE ruse to apply a test to love—both her own and that of her lover—to prove it true. A man would as soon as think of applying a match to a powder magazine to prove it combustible.

Love in woman's eyes is the supreme and ultimate arbitrator. If she is loved, love in her eyes will condone anything—anything. For

To prefer honor to love is a maxim to women unknown. With them love Is honor. And therefore the maxim is meaningless—and needless.

IT IS A SORT OF legal—or rather charitable—fiction that women should surrender only to love. In fact,

Do not even the lightest of Laises and Thaises make a show of being swayed by love? And

No woman by too much love was ever spoiled. Man, remember that!

THE LOGIC OF THE EMOTIONS differs from the logic of the intellect. As to the senses—

Alack-a-day! The senses never reason.

Love sometimes wrecks its barque upon the rocks to prove that they harbor no mirage.

Love sometimes forgets that it is possible to probe too far.

Love, in pursuit of love, sometimes vivisects as unconsciously as a science in pursuit of life.

WOMEN DETECT THE DAWN OF love while it is still midnight with a man. That is to say,

A woman knows a man is in love with her long before he is aware of it himself. Except perhaps in this once circumstance: when she herself is in love with somebody else. And this is a highly important circumstance.

WHOLLY TO SATISFY MASCULINE INFATUATION is given to no woman. And perhaps

Wholly to satisfy feminine caprice is given to no man. So, sometimes,

The last refuge of an unrequited love is the belief that love will create love. Nothing can be more futile than such a faith. Yet

Love without hope, has its mitigations; but

How alleviate the pain of a love that mistook a simulated love for a true one?

A simulated love is a contradiction in terms.

Either one loves or one does not, that is the conclusion of the whole matter.

LOVE WOULD RATHER SUFFER THAN forget.

Love would give the world to be able to exculpate a languid lover.

A passionate love is perhaps always poignant.

Love disdains pity.

A wounded love carries a scar to the grave.

IN LOVE, WHEN HONOR IS lost, loss of shame soon follows. Then indeed the downward patch becomes precipitous.

To some, love never comes; to some, it comes too often; but the same love never recurs, as never a bud opens twice: happy he or she is who gains bud, blossom, and fruit. Since

The sweetest love is that wherein the odorous flower of passion ripens into the nourishing fruitage of affection. But

Love requires careful nature. And

The more exotic the love, the more difficult its culture.—True, An orchid may life on air. Yes; but how torrid and vaporous an air!

Your sturdy mistletoe thrives on the humble apple; a Cattleya requires a Columbian forest.

Youth wonders at the amatory successes of middle-age. Youth knows not that

In matters amatory, age is no handicap:

A girl in her 'teens will make love to a gentleman of forty—and vice versa. In fact

The indiscreet impetuosity of youth succumbs before the astuteness of age.

The bachelor and the spinster both sometimes wonder that the benedick and the bride are still their rivals; for they know not that

In the amatorial art, matrimony is no handicap. In short,

There is no barrier at which love will balk. Nay more,

Love will forgive anything:

Did love demand it, love, though it might blush, would not blench. And

Often love itself stands amazed at its own divine audacity. Indeed,

Love loves to immolate itself for love. Knowing that

To love, nothing is common or unclean: for

Love, like charity, thinketh no evil. But—remember that

It is only the Uranian Aphrodite that dares essay a divine audacity. Nevertheless,

Love is the most vulnerable of the emotions, and

A love doubtful of itself would be cautiously accepted: it is not a fact that

To try to feel one's own pulse, is to make the heart beat irregularly? So,

To try to see in a mirror the love light in one's own eyes, is to be-dim it. So, too,

If passion is not linked with affection—woe worth the day when the troth was plighted! But given passion linked with affection—ah!

ARNOLD HAULTAIN

Nothing, nothing is criminal to love; for love knows not conscience. Or rather,

Love upsets all conventional conditions. For

Love creates a world of its own, a world populated by two—and these make their own laws—or make none. So

A woman will imbrue her hands with blood, and a man will fling honor to the winds, and yet the twain regard each other as impeccant and impeccable.—Till Pippa passes; then,

Love always awakes to the fact that not even a community of two can live without law; and that

Though human laws may be outraged, those divine may not. And assuredly,

The ideal love is the divine love. And, in ideal love,

Strange, strange, but true, in a great and ardent love, when at last that is offered which was long sought, there supervenes upon the lovers a great tenderness, which hesitates to make their own that for which they yearned. Almost it were as if

A psychic monitor warned the conqueror to be clement, and the captive to be kind. This

Tenderness is the worship of the soul by the soul. And

Of all tests of love tenderness is the truest. But indeed, indeed

In love there are heights above heights, depths beneath depths: who shall scale them, who shall plumb?

Chapter V

On Lovers

"Si vis amari ama."

—Seneca

Lovers think the world was made for them—and so perhaps it was.

To each other, lovers are the most interesting personages alive; but onlookers regard them partly with amusement, partly with pity, partly with compassion—in the etymological sense of that word.

The first wonder of every accepted lover is that he should be the accepted lover of such a woman.—What the woman thinks. . . what the woman thinks, probably not even she herself knows. Probably each woman thinks her own thoughts.

To doubt whether one is in love is to prove oneself out of it.

To impress upon the lover the still-existing necessity of refining gold or painting the lily is out of the question. Yet every woman attempts it.

If there is one proverb more distasteful than another to a hotheaded lover, it is that half a loaf is better than no bread.

Children, dogs, and old people are difficult to deceive. Lovers who have to use circumspection should remember this.

A doubting lover should mark how, and for whom, his woman dresses.

To die for a woman would perhaps, to a young and ardent lover, not be difficult; to wage incessant warfare with the world for her, that perhaps is not so easy. But it is the better test of love; and perhaps also the better preserver and replenisher of love. For

Little as people seem to be aware of it, love requires constant replenishing: no flame can burn without a feeding oil, no pool overflow with out a purling brook. Yet

The first ecstasies of love often blind both lover and lass to the care necessary for the nurture of love. Indeed,

To many treat love as if it were a passing whim; whereas in sober reality it is (or should be) a lasting emotion.

Love, with woman, is like the tides. And

Few women know the high-water mark of their love: they are always harboring the belief that it may rise still higher; and often they await that rise.

It is but the reflection of himself in his mistress that many a foolish lover loves.

That aged spinster is a rare one who does not regret she did not accept one of her lovers. But

That younger spinster is not to be envied who has to make choice of several.

Youth glories in the multiplicity of its lovers; age sometimes wishes it had had but one.

The unloved think lad the one thing needful. The beloved know that an ocean of love could be swallowed up and the parched soul cry out athirst.

It is not well either to confide or confess too much.

A very small rock will wreck a very big ship, and a very small slip will spoil a very long life.

The pain which lovers cause each other—through fickleness, languidness, jealousy, and the thousand natural shocks that love is heir to—is not altogether pain, though at the moment it may seem the most poignant anguish the human soul could suffer. One proof of this lies in the fact that

There are few who would choose to have missed love's pangs altogether.

Perhaps the pleasure intermixed with love's pangs arises from the thought that the other is the cause of our suffering. For,

In all love, it is the sacrifice of oneself for the other that brings keenest joy. And yet

There is an element of self-love in the very extremest of love. Since

Love, after all, is a debtor and creditor affair. (Who ever loved with no hope of return?) It is when one of the parties declares him-or herself insolvent that the account is closed—with many tears and sighs on the part of the chief creditor. At all events

The intenser the love, the more flawless does its object appear. For

The surest test of the sincerity of love is that it thinketh no evil.

The surest test of a waning love is that it begins not to content itself when it sees its object suffer.

The surest test of a dead love is that it forgets how to be jealous.

THE FALLING-OUT OF LOVERS TRUE is a renewing may be of love. Still it is not to be recommended. In fact, it might be said that

Every falling-out of lovers true is a nail in love's coffin. Yet,

A blessing it is that in love we remember the sweet rather than the bitter. For

Love was ever bitter-sweet.

THE HEART OF A LOVER is like that bottom of a well: all the beauties of the starry heavens are revealed in it; but when it sheds the light of its countenance upon it, all else is obliterated.

WAS ANY LOVER EVER LOVED enough? Or

Did any ever hear of a tired lover? Nevertheless often

"Drink to me only with thine eyes", says the youthful lover; but when the seance is over he goes out and orders beef-steak and bottled beer.

WHAT IT REALLY CRAVES, THE lover's heart is impotent to express. Yet, it is ever attempting.

A lover is full of wishes as an egg is full of meat. But

What it really wishes no lover seems able to say. As a matter of fact,

The endless task which the lover is ever attempting is a search for a formula for the summation of an infinite series of which love is the variable.—Few lovers seem to understand this.

To KINDLE ASPIRATION IN HER lover, a woman herself need not be aspiring. For,

Whatever the talents of a man, they are stimulated by contact with woman. Since

An elevating influence seems to radiate from women: we have but to come into the light of their countenances for our own faces to shine as the sun. Indeed,

Physicists may talk as they like, but lovers know a more subtle and a more potent force than any yet revealed to them. It has not yet been named; but for the present it might be called "psychicity".

IF YOU WISH TO ASCERTAIN the relationship of a youthful pair, watch their eyes. For

Simulation is difficult to the eye.

WHEN THE IDOL INTO WHICH a woman has converted her lover is dethroned, she still worships her remembrance of her god, and puts together and treasures the broken pieces.

When the idol into which has converted his loved one is dethroned, he generally changes his creed.

A CIRCUMPSECTING LOVER IS A woman's abhorrence: as a calculating mistress is a man's.

LET A LOVER BUT PUT himself into the hands of his mistress, and he is safe. Since

The man she really loves, a woman will shield through thick and thin, through right and wrong. For,

Concerning a man, the only question a woman asks is, not, "Is he right or wrong?" but, "Is he mine or another's?"—We men therefore

Leave a woman to get her lover out of a scrape.

IT IS TO BE FEARED that the men and women who love but once and forever are not usually to be found outside of romances.

With women, love is a river, ever-flowing, from the brook in girlhood, to the estuary of womanhood. Like a river, too,

Woman's love is fed by all the streams it meets. On the other hand,

With man, love is a geyser.

THE LANGUISHING LOVER HAS GONE out of date; he has been replaced by the diverting one. And the change is significant of much: The early nineteenth-century maid pretended to ignorance; the early twentieth-century maid to omniscience.

The early nineteenth-century suitor protested; but

The early twentieth-century suitor has to contest. In the one case,

The woman tacitly acknowledges an inequality. In the other case,

The man has to openly to recognize his equal. Nevertheless,

The fundamental relationship between the sexes do not materially vary from century to century, much as conventional manners and customs may. For, after all,

Always what a man seeks in a woman is: love. And

In all love there is something perfectly and Paradisiacally pristine.

Would the most emancipated woman have love otherwise? At all events,

Perhaps the most womanly position a woman can occupy is: with her head on her lover's heart. At this the strong-minded may scoff. They may.

THE OBSESSION OF THE MALE heart by one woman ousts from it all other women. Thus,

The accepted young man regards all women but the one as he would regard fashion-plates. To the young woman men continue to be men. That is to say,

A man dives headlong into love. A woman paddles into it. And the woman's hesitation at the brink of the stream exasperates the spluttering man. In short,

A man's heart is captured wholly and at a stroke. A woman's heart surrenders itself piecemeal.

Whereas, with a man, a trivial passion is usually an affair more of the senses or of the imagination than of the heart; with a woman every passions is an affair of the heart.

A man, when first he is in love, is absorbed in the contemplation of the object of his love. A woman is similarly situated is capable of making comparisons.

It gives to woman's curiosity a curious pleasure to compare the methods of men's proposals.

In love, a woman is generally cool enough to calculate pros and cons; a man, in similar plight, is incapable of anything but folly.

It is a feminine motto that a woman needs to be taught how to love. Perhaps she does; but most men will think one private tutor ought to suffice, and that tutor ought to be he. At all events,

The last schoolmaster would be apt to regard with somewhat mixed feelings the tuition of previous crammers.

Why go to the trouble of explaining away a first love, if the second is no whit its inferior? Unless it be to overcome.

What a second love chiefly deplores is: that it was not he (or she) who first taught his (or her) loved one to love. Is it not true also that

It is the first love that amazes, that beautifies, that consecrates?

(An illicit love beautifies and consecrates nothing:

A Maud leaves the daisies rosy; not so Faustine.)

Many a woman has given her heart to one lover and herself to another. The first is always won; the second is sometimes extorted. Yet,

It is wonderful how a woman will contrive to make all her lovers believe they are winners.

It often gives a lady a pleasure to give her lover a pang.

Not many but have tasted the bitterness of the conflict between the desire of the flesh and the resentment of the spirit. Explain these terms who may.

To attempt by erring to cure an erring lover, is to administer, not an antidote, but an adjuvant. It works poison in the blood. When (and if) in a tortuous love, a man arrives at a 'Don't give a damn' stage, he is not to be classed with the animals known as docile. And as to a woman. . . but polite language has its limits.

Many a man has be exasperated, not only by the audacity of his rival, but by the equanimity with which his lady-love views that audacity. He forgets that, as a rule,

Feminine complaisance varies directly as masculine audacity. And yet, often enough, as a simple matter of fact, Masculine diffidence is vastly more potent than masculine audacity. And further,

Rarely need the complaisance that audacity evokes perturb the diffident man; since

Rarely need the complaisance that audacity evokes perturb the diffident man; since

The true woman may give her fingertips to the gallant; she gives herself to the worshiper. The pity o' it is that

The worshiper cannot away with the complaisance that permits a woman to give even her finger-tips to the gallant. And

Few are the women who have plumbed the silent and sensitive depths of the diffidence of her devotee. The worst of it is,

The devotee essays two things: he would apotheosize the object of his adoration and place her as a constellation among the stars; yet he would have her at the same time terrestrial and tangible. When the woman shows herself terrestrial and tangible to others than he, the faith of the devotee is shaken. In fine,

Every lover attempts that impossible task: the realization of the heavenly ideal. Perhaps

It is in aphelion that the corona appears most splendid;

Were perihelion to result is coalescence, perhaps the photosphere would be proved composed of terrestrial vapors. And if it did (as no doubt it would), would it be at all bedimmed? For, to the devout astrologer

Nothing, nothing will ever destroy beauty—and therefore wonder. So,

Bodily beauty, where Love is priestess, is a daedal spur to the loftiest worship.

The lover is ever worshipful. And

Where is worship, nothing can be profane. So

In love there is nor taint nor stain. Therefore,

Make, O youthful lover, the best and most of youth and love: never will either recur.

Chapter VI

On Making Love

"Mille modi Veneris"

—Ovid

There are as many ways of making love as there are of making soup. And probably

There are as many kinds of love as there are of flavors. And

Palates—both sentimental and physical—evidently differ widely. And yet,

If you would know the secret of success with women, it is said in a word: Ardor. And

Would ye, O women, know in a word the secret of success with men? It lies in: Responsiveness.

In matters amatory—or rather pre-amatory—feminine tactics are infallible and consummate:

Let no man think to cope with feminine strategy.

A rake has more chance than a ninny.—Which doubtless has been said before.

In love, as in all things, indecision spells ruination. For

There is a curious antagonism between the sexes. They are in a manner foes, not friends. The successful wooer is the captor, the raptor; the bride is the capture, the rapture. And

Even she who is minded to be caught will not spare her huntsman the ardor of the chase, and lightly esteems him who imagines she is to be lightly won.

In the chess-like game of love-making, no woman plays for check-mate: the game interests her too much to bring it to a finish. What pleases her most is stale-mate, where, though the King cannot be captured, the captress can maneuver without end.

A man imagines he wins by strenuous assault. The woman knows the victory was due to surrender.

WOULDST THOU ASK OUGHT OF a woman? Question her eyes: they are vastly more voluble than her tongue. Indeed,

There is no question too subtle, too delicate, too recondite, or too rash, for human eyes to ask or answer. And

He who has not learned the language of the eyes, has yet to learn the alphabet of love. Besides,

Love speaks two languages: one with the lips; the other with the eyes. (There is really a third; but this is Pentecostal.) At all events,

Lovers always talk in a cryptic tongue.

There is but one universal language: the ocular—not Volapuk nor Esperanto is as intelligible or as efficacious as this.

NO WOMAN CAN BE COERCED into love,—though she may be coerced into marriage. And

Man, the clumsy wielder of one blunt weapon, often enough stands agape at his own powerlessness before the invulnerable woman of his desire. Indeed,

The battle between the coquettish maid and determined man is like the battle between the Retiarius and the Mirmillio. The coquetry ensnares the man as with a net against which his sword is useless.

A WOMAN'S EMOTIONS ARE AS practical as a man's reason.

A man's emotions are never practical. This is why,

In the emotional matter of love, men and women so often lash. And perhaps

It is a beneficial thing for the race that a woman's emotions are practical. For

If neither the man nor the woman curbed the mettlesome Pegasus "Emotion", methinks the colts and fillies would want for hay and oats.

IT IS A MOOT QUESTION which is the more fatally fascinating: the uniformed nurse or the weeded widow. But

Who has yet discovered the secret springs of fascination? For example,

How is it that certain eyes and lips will enthrall, while others leave us cold and inert?

Does the potency lie in the eyes and the lips, or is there some inscrutable and psychic power? At all events, who will explain how it is that

A man will sometimes forsake the most beautiful of wives and a woman will forsake the kindest of husbands to follow recklessly one who admits no comparison with the one forsaken? All we can say is that

The potency of personality exceeds the potency of beauty. For, Powerful as is physical charm, it counts not for all in the matter of love. Yet what it may be that does count, and how and why it does count, no man living shall say. For

Is even love aware of all its seeks? And

Is it given to any to grant all that love beseeches? And yet

Were all love sought bestowed, what sequel?

Perhaps 't were well to leave love but semi-satisfied. At bottom the real question is this: What will win and keep me another heart? But

How to win and keep another heart, that is a thing has to be found out for oneself—if it be discoverable. And always by the experimental method. Since

In matters amatory, there is no a priori reasoning possible. All we know is that

There is nothing more potent than passion. And

The chasm, which seems to innocence to yawn between virtue and frailty, is leapt by that Pegasus, Passion, at a bound—but he blinds his rider in the feat.

IN SPITE OF THE POESY of love, deeds are more potent than words;— though perhaps it is well to pave the way for the one by the other.

In spite, too of the piety of love, love laughs at promises—that is, the promises that affect it.

THERE IS ONE MIRACLE THAT women can always perform, and always it astonishes the man; it is this: to change from the recipient into the appellant. That is to say,

When woman, usually regarded as the receiver, becomes the giver,— or rather the demander,—man's wonderment surpasses words. And let it be remembered that

There is no re-crossing this Rubicon.

MISTRUST A PROLONGED AND OBDURATE resistance. Either you are out-classed, or you are out-experienced. And, besides,

Surrender after prolonged resistance rarely is brought about by emotion.

A WOMAN NEVER REALLY QUITE detests daring. This is why Much is a forgiving a daring man. So, too,

Much is forgiven a pretty woman—by the men.

IF THE BEGINNING OF STRIFE is as when one letteth out water, the beginning of love is as when one kindleth a fire.

THE EYE TELLS MORE THAN the tongue. And

If the eye and the tongue contradict each other, believe the eye.

THERE IS AN INDIFFERENCE THAT attracts, and there is an indifference that repels. He is a sagacious man, and she is a sagacious woman, who will differentiate them. The question resolves itself into that which so often puzzles the angler,—how much line to let out. About one thing there need be no hesitation,

When your fish is within reach, be quick with the landing-net—or even with the gaff.

IN THE MATTER OF WOOING, soon enough does the young girl learn to prefer the mature manners of the man of the world to the gaucheries of inexperienced youth. As to the man!

How curious the things that appeal to this lord of creation, Man!—a half-averted face—a laughing gesture—a merry eye—an all but imperceptible tone of the voice—the scarce felt touch of a reluctant hand—a semi-tender phrase—an unexpected glance—the momentary pressure of petulant lips—a blanched cheek—a look prolonged one fractional part of a second beyond its wont—an infinitesimal drooping of the eyelid—a speaking silence—a half-caught sigh—these will entrap the male brute where green widths that were never dried will not hold him. But

By what men are won, most women seem thoroughly to comprehend.

By what women are won, few men know. Perhaps

No woman knows by what she herself is won.

One thing there is, at all events, to which woman will always succumb: tenderness. But remember, Dames, that

Tenderness is extremely difficult of simulation. Or rather,

Tenderness is so delicate and deep-seated a feeling, that few care to attempt its simulation.

A WOMAN WHO GIVES HERSELF too freely is apt to regret the giving. In time, too, she discovers that, as a matter of fact,

No woman can give her real self twice: one or other gift will prove to be a loan. (And

It is always and only the first recipient that causes a woman's heart to flutter, and often it flutters long.)

A second gift is generally a mortgage—if it is not a sale.

A mortgage is difficult to bind. For

There is a statute of limitations in love as there is in law. Nor is the former to be set aside by bond.

That pair is in a parlous state when either party discovers that the title was not properly searched. Since

Everybody expects a fee simple,—though few deserve it, God wot!

PERHAPS THE MOST DURABLE CONQUEST is the incomplete one. Which sounds illogical. But it is well to remember that

Repletion seems to cause, in the man, temporary indifference; while

Repletion causes, in the woman, enduring content. And in this we can detect a significant distinction between the sexes: namely the fact that

A single goal satisfies most women;

No single goal ever yet satisfied the restless spirit of man.

WHAT GIVES KEENEST JOY IS the evocation of latent passion. For Each takes pleasure in believing that he or she alone can evoke this passion. Accordingly,

The premature confession of passion, and the confession of premature passion, both rankle in the breast—and, probably, in the breast of both penitent and confessor.

WHAT INTENSITY OF FEELING a woman can throw into the enunciation of a Christian name! There is perhaps no better clue to possession that this. For, probably,

Not until a man's Christian mane is ecstatically uttered is a woman wholly his.

Men and women content with the different weapons. This is why Men are rarely intrepid in the presence of women; but women rarely stand in awe of men.—Nothing differentiates the sexes more than this; but the psychological reason is difficult to discover. Perhaps,

The making of love is a sort of duel, the conditions of which are that the man shall doff all his armor and the woman may don all hers. Indeed,

The battle of love-making would be an unequal combat, even were both contestants fully panoplied; for,

A woman's derision will pierce any mail. In fact,

No armor is impervious to woman's shafts—be they those of laughter or be they those of love. So

The veriest roué' is vulnerable to the veriest maid. But

For each man she meets, a woman carries in her quiver but one shaft. If that misses its aim, she is powerless: it is like a dart without a thong; when thrown, the man can close. But

Always it devolves upon the man to take the initiative. But, again,

Always the man must pretend that he takes no initiative. But, again,

Always the woman must pretend that she gives no opportunity.

The game of love is not only one of chance but one of skill. What irks man is that a woman pretends that she must be circumvented by wiles. But

Man was ever a clumsy wooer. Nevertheless,

It is only the man who thinks he is too venturesome. Since

The iciest woman sometimes thaws. And

The austerer a woman, the sweeter her surrender. And, again, A woman is never sweeter than in surrender. Accordingly,

"De l'audace, et encore de l'audace, et toujours de l'audace" should be the motto of every wooer. Since

Audacity if beloved of women; but it must be an audacity born of Sincerity and educated b y Discretion. At all events

Beware timidity,—it is fatal.

With women, nothing is more conquering than conquest; nothing so irresistible as resistance. On the other hand,

Resistance on the part of the woman is an effort put forth for the purpose of defeating its own object.

A man prizes only what he has fought for. No one knows this better than a woman. This is why

A woman's capitulation she always makes to appear as a capture. And

Where there are no defense works, a woman will erect them.

Foolish that man who does not storm entrenchments. For

Resistance on the part of a woman is a wall which a man is expected to leap. His agility is the measure of her approbation.

AROUSE A WOMAN'S INTEREST, AND you arouse much. But Having failed, disappear. Yet

It takes very many futile attempts to make a failure. At the same time,

Importunity is an inferior weapon.

A CONDITIONAL SURRENDER IS NO surrender. But

A woman's surrender is in reality a desertion, a going over to the enemy. Thenceforward she is an ally. Indeed

A woman's capitulation is her conquest.

LET NO AMOUNT OF SIMULATED austerity deter you. The marble Galatea came to life at the prayer of a man.

THE NUMBER OF MODES IN which a woman can say 'Yes' has not, up to the present, be accurately enumerated; but perhaps the one most frequently in use is the negative imperative. And

Many are the men who have puzzled long and painfully over the motives of a woman's 'No.' Yet in nine cases out of ten a woman says 'No' merely because she feels herself on the brink of saying 'Yes'. In other words,

It is often mistrust of herself that leads many a woman to refuse it will the lips the consent that is fluttering at her heart. Perhaps that is why

With woman 'Yea' and 'Nay' are meaningless and interchangeable terms.

'WARE A SHOW OF EXCESSIVE feeling. It is proof, either that it is shallow and evanescent, or that it is put on. At all events Excessive feeling is rarely taken seriously. Now

Seriousness adds a spice to gallantry. But, like spice, a little is ample.

MANY MEN THINK IT IS the woman who has to be persuaded. It is not the woman; it is her scruples. Besides, "Nemo repente turpissimus—vel turpissima". Yet

By thirty, scruples are either dormant or dominant.

Both of the callow youth of fifteen and the man of the world of forty-five swear by the woman of thirty.

It may seem a paradox, but it is a truism, that, in matters of love, it is the weaker and the defenseless sex that takes the initiative. In other words,

The woman makes the opportunity which the man takes. And

An opportunity missed is an opportunity lost. And

The woman is implacable to the man who sees the opportunity and takes it not. Since

With woman indifference is worse than insult. Wherefore

Never, never disappoint a woman.

Spontaneous admiration is the sincerest flattery. Those who know this, affect spontaneity. But it requires much art to conceal this art.

You will oftener err upon the side of ultra-delicacy in a compliment that upon the side of bare-facedness.

Do not imagine that excessive admiration can give offence. But remember that

The eye can netter express admiration than can the tongue.

The publicity with which a woman will receive admiration from a male admirer 144 often is sufficient to astonish that admirer. But

Often enough it is the admiration, not the admirer, that a woman covets. Indeed,

Many a woman is in love with love, but not her lover. But this no lover can be got to comprehend.

To flatter by deprecating a rival is a complement of extremely doubtful efficacy.

A woman does not admire too clement a conqueror. She admits the right to ovation, and to him who waives it she lightly regards.

Seek no stepping-stones unless you mean to cross:

He who gathers stepping-stones and refrains from crossing is contempted of women. Indeed,

Every advance of which advantage is not taken, is in reality a retreat. And remember, too, that though

Sought interviews are sweet, those unsought are sweeter. And

Probably no son of Adam—and for the matter of that, probably no daughter of Eve—ever quite looks back with remorse upon a semi-innocent escapade. Yet

The man who thinks he can at any time extract himself from any feminine entanglement that he may choose to have raveled, is a simpleton.

THE WAY OF MAN WITH a maid may have been too wonderful for Agur; now-a-days the way of a man with a married woman would puzzle a wiser than he.

What is the attitude to be maintained towards the too complaisant spouse of an honorable friend? That is a problem will puzzle weak men without end. Of that fatal and fateful dilemma when a wife or a husband falls victim to the wiles of another, there are, for the delinquent, two and only two horns (and it is a moot question upon which it is preferable to be impaled): Flight—either from the victor or the victrix. Yet

To some it is no anomaly to pray God's blessing upon a liaison. But these folk are to be pitied; for

A clandestine love always works havoc—havoc to all three.

Will men and women never learn what trouble they lay up in store for themselves by breaking their plighted troths?

Chapter VII

On Beauty

"La beaute' pour moi c'est la divinite' visible, c'est le bonheur palpable, c'est le ciel descendu sur terre."

—THEOPHILE GAUTIER

B eauty, they say, is but skin-deep. That is quite deep enough to enslave mankind. As a matter of fact, it is much deeper: for, to say nothing of health and good-spirits,

Beneath true beauty lies an admirable or a loveable character. And yet—or, perhaps, and therefore—

If by some mischance beauty should arouse our resentment, with what different eyes we regard it!

THE FEELING FOR BEAUTY IS probably more highly developed in man than in woman. (N. B. Perhaps this is the source of the beauty of women.) Nevertheless,

It is a question that perhaps will never be settled, how much value should be placed upon mere beauty. For

Man soon tires of mere beauty. In fact, man, the inconstant creature, soon tires of mere anything.

BEAUTY SHOULD NEVER BE ANALYZED. At sight of graceful neck, who speaks of "musculus sterno-cleido-mastoideus"; at touch of moist red lips, who thinks upon the corpuscles of Paccini?

MORE WOMEN ARE WOOED FOR their complexions than for their characters.

COULD WOMEN ONLY KNOW IT, nothing can add to their charms: how provokingly delightful is the uniformed demureness of an hospital nurse beside the elaborate bedizenments of a woman of fashion!

THE MOST BEAUTIFUL THING KNOWN among men is: a good woman. And this is not an anomaly.

SHE WHO CAPTURES A MAN by a single charm, be it even beauty, holds him by a weak chain.

Think not it was merely beauty that made Helen or Cleopatra historic.

Beauty is much, and grace is much; but there is a charm more subtle and potent than these.

BEAUTY WITHOUT MODESTY IS A rose without perfume: the petals may delight, but they lack an ineffable savor. Like a flower, too,

Though the tangible petals are numbered and comptable, the subtle perfume eludes the sense and is inexhaustible. For

Modesty is the exhalation of the soul: at once it enhances, as it refines, the potency of beauty. Nay more,

The sacrosanct aureole of modesty beautifies all it surrounds: though it diviner haze imperfection there is none. So,

Given a redolent balm, and the lowliest herb becomes treasured and precious. And

Each human soul has its own individual essence;

What folly were the violet to envy the rose! Since

Beauty is much, and grace is much, and mien and demeanor and wit; but a prepotent and psychic essence there is transcending the power of these. And,

As the suave and subtle essence is not distinct from, but springs from, the tangible and numerable petals, so the spirit perceives that its fleshy vesture is not a thing apart, to be donned or doffed at will, to b e contemned or left out of regards, but indeed at integral and inseparable portion of itself; for

In the very woof and warp of flesh, sprit is immanent and enmeshed. Indeed—though in a mystic sense—

Vesture and wearer are mutually one. And yet

Love ever essays the task of seeking out the psychic wearer beneath the corporeal vesture—often with plaintive strife.

When seeker and sought make a mutual search—the starkest strife is condoned. But alack!

The mystic unity of the human soul is never wholly divulged—not even to love—not even to love.

Chapter VIII

On Courtship

"Un amant fait la court ou s'attache son coeur".

—Moliere

A woman really in love and sure of her lover delights in toying with a sort of coquetry of love; as if it pleased her to try to win over again that the winning of which gave so exquisite a pleasure. And perhaps

The coquetry of love is the surest test of an unquestionable love. For

When possession can afford to play at pursuit, this but proves possession complete. Sometimes

An assumed love will resort to the pretty tricks of a real one, in order to assure its object—or to re-assure itself.

Surrender after a protracted siege has its advantages. At all events both *M* and *N* can look back to more demi-semi happy incidents when the courtship has been long.

Happy that couple can laugh over the incidents of courtship afterwards. 'T is a portent of impending ill if they cannot.

Half-heartedness in courtship is not only suicidal, it is murderous. On the other hand, remember that

In courtship there are various and varying stages. But there is always the home-gallop. Remember, too, that

What is suitable at one stage of courtship is ruinous at another. And

It is only the old whip who knows when to push the pace:

In courtship to force the running is hazardous. Though we win, the victory loses its sweets. And

In courtship, men too often ride on the snaffle; in matrimony, too often on the curb.

Courtship asks for cash payment. Matrimony has often to allow unlimited credit. Insolvency is not unknown.

In courtship, all auxiliaries but the rival. No one will impede a lover save another lover.

In the presence of a woman, man is by nature a diffident animal. The women who recognize this are often the most successful. Indeed,

Many are the refined and gentle women who in after life regret that they did not more openly cope with their less delicately-minded sisters. Nevertheless,

Nothing is more astonishing than a woman's tact in encouraging a man.

In courtship modulated and musical tones count for much. Who with harsh speech would assail a lady's ear?

No woman thinks she can be wooed too often. And

Few women can forgo an opportunity to fascinate.

In courtship the woman is the whole world to the man; in matrimony the man is the whole world to the woman.

In courtship the slightest suspicion of condescension is fatal. For

True love is a greater leveler than anarchy.

In courtship, the wooer to the wooed is, in Juliet's phrase, the god of her idolatry; in matrimony he is lucky if he is the idol of her deity.

It is a question which is the sweeter: a spontaneous courtship, or one that has sprung from friendship.

In a spontaneous courtship there is all the charm of novelty;

In a courtship that has grown out of affection there is all the trustfulness of friendship. But

Friendship and courtship are two totally distinct things:

In courtship, men and women meet on the flowery-thorny common of love;

In friendship, men and women invite each other over to their respective plots. So,

A friend will show a friend all over his domain;

A lover can but point out to the lover the flowers (and thorns) which grow in the soil to which they are both strangers.

It is an open question whether in matters pre-matrimonial, the mode of the French is not preferable to that of the Anglo-Saxon; whether, that is,

Prudence and prevision are not more certain harbingers of matrimonial happiness of matrimonial happiness than are impulse and passion.

The French couple, when wedded, are virtually strangers; the Anglo-Saxon have already together enacted some scenes of the matrimonial drama. Yet it is an open question also whether

A more durable domestic affection is not built up from the pristine foundation of total ignorance than from that of a partial acquaintanceship.

The American Elizabeth Patterson, before she became Madame Jerome Bonaparte, could write, "I love Jerome Bonaparte, and I prefer to be his wife, were it only for a day, to the happiest union."

The continentalized Madame Jerome Bonaparte, twenty-six years after she had ceased to be Miss Elizabeth Patterson, could write "Do we not know how easily men and women free themselves from the fetters of love, and that only the stupid remain caught in these pretended bonds?" After all,

Little do any couple know of each other before marriage. Besides Does not a delightful romance envelope the nuptials of strangers? At all events, even if precaution is a foe to impulse, few will be found to deny that

Strangeness is by no means inimical to passion. Perhaps, then, Fathers and mothers and uncles and aunts can form a better judgment as to the suitability and adaptability to each other of two young, ardent, and headstrong boys and girls can these themselves; since

Fathers and mothers and uncles and aunts know full well that impulse and passion often prove materials too friable for the many-storied fabric of marriage. At all events,

The French mode of contracting a marriage precludes the possibility of perilous and precocious affairs of the heart. Perhaps

The mistake that ardent and headstrong boys and girls make is in thinking that impulse and passion are the keys of Paradise. Their Elders know that impulse and passion are sometimes the keys of Purgatory.

Prudence and prevision are not keys to any supernal (or infernal) existence; they are merely guide-books to a terrestrial journey. At all events, it is significant that (which might be added as a lemma)

Widows rarely choose unwisely!

OVER THAT MUCH-BETHOUGHT-OF, much-surmised-about-thing, a proposal of marriage, every young woman weaves a pre-conceived halo of romance, but

In nineteen cases out of twenty a proposal is either unexpected or disappointing; that is,

Many a girl has almost held her breath with anxiety as she saw the great question coming; then almost cried with vexation at the way it came. For, often,

Either the wrong man proposes or the right man proposes stupidly.

The woman looks for ideal surroundings, a dramatic situation, and impassioned and poetic utterance; usually,

The man seizes a commonplace opportunity and—stutters. Probably,

The ideal proposal occurs only in novels. And yet—and yet—

Perhaps after all the real proposal is more complimentary to woman than is the ideal; at least perhaps

The aberration and obfuscation of the man is proof once *(i)* of her potency and *(ii)* of his sincerity.

Did man keep his head, would woman be quite so sure of his heart? Yet it may be that in these matter woman is liable to err, since

Rarely, if ever, does a woman's heart run away with her head. When it does—

Ah! the momentary bliss of an unreasoning emotion! Yet

Woman does right to keep her head, for

Almost every woman's happiness depends upon what she does with her heart—unless indeed she elects to go through life homeless, childless, and unenspoused; for

Though it is the wife that makes the home, it is the man who must provide for it. And since

Man, by nature, is probably nomadic and polygamic; not his to debate whether to give rein to emotion. Woman, by nature, is in far different case:

For the sake of her child, woman must bind the nomad to herself. Accordingly,

It is woman who is the true agglutinator and civilizer of society. Therefore, it comes about that

To order wisely her emotions is the inherited instinct of woman. Wherefore,

Woman is the conserver of the nation—and this in more senses than one.

Chapter IX

On Men and Women

"Dio fa gli uomini, e e' s' appaino."

—SALVIATI

There are two elements of character which a man should possess, develop, and maintain unstained if he would find favor in feminine eyes: the first is bravery; the second, indomitableness of resolution. So likewise,

There are two elements of character which a woman should possess, develop, and maintain unstained if she would find favor in masculine eyes: the first is sympathy; the second, sweetness of temper.

A CURIOUS AND LATENT HOSTILITY divides the sexes. It seems as they could not approach each other without alarums and excursions. Always the presence of the one rouses anxiety in the breast of the other; they stand to arms; they resort to tactics; they maneuver. And,

Men and women approach each other vizored and in armor. But it is often only to conceal the craven heart that beats beneath the brazen cuirass.

MEN JUDGE OF WOMEN, NOT so much by their intrinsic worth, as by the impression women make upon them. And women know this, since All women are alive to the fact that the impressing of men is the important function of life. Accordingly,

Great stress is, and is naturally, laid by women upon dress and the subtleties of the toilette. For,

In matters of the heart man is led by the heart and not by the head. And why not? Since

It is generally a sweet-heart, not a hard head, that a man wants. In short,

Men are oftener vanquished by a look than by logic; by a gracious smile than by good sense; by manner and even by dress than by mental development or depth. This is to say,

A man judges a woman by her appearance;

A woman judges a woman by her motives. (And

A woman judges of a woman's motives by what she knows of her own.)—So it comes about that,

To a man, a woman's heart is something mysterious. But

Women, who know their own hearts, have little difficulty in reading others'.

No units of measurement yet devised are adequate for the computation of the power wielded by a beautiful woman.

That is a significant fact, and probably, could we fathom all the profundities and unravel all the entanglements of the relations between the sexes, as deep and as intricate as significant, that no woman thinks a man can pay her a higher compliment than to wish to make her his own. For though

Woman thinks man her ultimate aim and desire, Nature knows that man is but the stepping-stone to the child. In the end woman agrees with Nature. We may go farther, and say

Women are nearer the eternal laws than are men. Men govern themselves by the laws they themselves make. Women are lawless. Laws are for the temporal, the fleeting; for a given individual in a given society; for a particular race in a particular clime. Such laws are obeyed by women only under compulsion. They, more far-seeing than men, instinctively peer far beyond the ephemeral rules manufactured by men, into the realm of laws eternal and immutable; these she obeys implicitly, unquestioningly—much to man's amazement—and, it may be, his mortification; for he sees that she is freer than he. This is why,

For the man she truly loves a woman will sacrifice everything—everything. The same generous sentiment cannot by any means be attributed to man.

Both the wise man and the wise woman—but here I am reminded of the recipe for hare soup.

Between the sexes there is in reality but one link—the link amatory. And

So long as Nature maintains two sexes, so long will men and women hug, yet chafe under, that slender but invisible bond.

Not even Cupid and Psyche avoided a misunderstanding—in spite of the devotion of the other. And,

If men and women differ in matters amatory, it is because men and women have trodden different evolutionary paths:

The man, given up to the chase (for pelts or pelf) and careful of his status in the tribe, thinks only of himself and the present;

The woman, her sole care the nurture of her offspring, thinks only of her progeny, and the future. But since

The family is the unit of the state, therefore

The state makes laws, not for love, but for the family.

Happy that family the parents of which are bound by cosmic not by municipal affection. Nevertheless,

Say what one will, Love scoffs at laws; howsoever marriage and divorce may be regulated by parliamentary statute.

Man, as a member of a political community, may make marriage laws to suit that community—laws to suit that community—laws "de vinculo matrimonii" and laws "de mensa et thoro", decrees "nisi prius" and decrees absolute; but

Law can no more bind the affections than it can bind the sweet influences of the Pleiades. And yet, at bottom,

Beneath all municipal and parochial regulations, a great and cosmic law does govern the relations of the sexes; and

The lightest whim of the lightest lady has a definite, perhaps a cosmic, fount and origin.

A MAN CAN NEVER KNOW too much. Perhaps a woman can. And

It is a question how far a man admires a woman who knows too much. For,

If there is nothing a man can teach a woman, not even of the ways of love, the man is apt to be chagrined. Besides,

Too much knowledge is inimical to romance.

WAR IS A MAN'S TRUE trade; love, woman's.

THERE IS NO STRONGER ARGUMENT against the equality of the sexes than a woman's hand. It was made to toil? No; to place in her lover's. In truth,

Is there anything more fragile in nature than a woman's hand? But put it in her lover's. and what a force it has!

Anomaly of anomalies, with women, fragility, delicacy, dependence, beauty, grace,—it is by these weak weapons that she wins. So,

We watch a demure damsel of some sixteen sunny summers much as we watch a delicate dynamo of some thousand kilowatts.

Both seem so calm, so quiescent. Yet both, we know, can generate such startling energy, can bring about such marvelous results.

MANY WOMEN FORGET THAT THINGS which men have no objection to their female friends doing they often have a very particular objection to their mothers, sisters, and wives doing. So, too, they often forget that

It is not the girl he flatters, compliments, and is conspicuously attentive to, that the man always marries. Perhaps this goes to show that

There is a deeper and more serious current in the flow of male emotions, which, much as light and fitful breezes may stir the surface, is moved only by, and mingles only, with a similar and confluent stream. For

It is not man's highest instincts that are stimulated by the more superficial of feminine blandishments; though, no doubt, many a man there is has been made permanently captive by their lure. The truth is that

Man is a many-sided creature: he will reflect many different rays; but it is only under the ray that pierces the surface and irradiates the interior that he truly glows.

WOMAN DOES NOT LEAN UPON man because she is inferior, but rather because she is his supporter; just as

The buttress leans upon the building; but the building would fall without the buttress. That is,

Woman's dependence upon man is his chief source of strength. Those who cannot understand this may be left to their ignorance.

IT IS NOT ALL WOMEN who comprehend the exaltation of mind into which some men are thrown by their presence. Indeed,

Men put a higher value upon a woman's complaisance than she does herself. To a women, feminine concession appear trivial. Is it any wonder, then, that

Woman calls man's jealousy unreasonable? In reality,

The affianced man thinks he has gotten him an angel from heaven. It is not within the bounds of mortal male comprehension that such an angel should sully her wings.

WOMEN KNOW THEIR SEX.—WHICH, if it is a truism, is a truism that men often forget. And

Few things permit a man to see so far into the subtleties and intricacies of feminine hearts as a squabble between two of them over himself.

A MAN IN DEFEAT GENERALLY turns to woman. A woman in defeat is either scornful, silent, or both.

A man, in depression, falls back upon his only weapon: brute force. A woman, in like circumstances, does the same. But her weapon is personal charm.

IN MATTERS AMATORY AND MATERNAL, a woman will risk more than will a man. In fact,

In matters amatory and maternal, woman is the truly combative animal.

MANY ARE THE MEMBERS OF the one sex that are entrapped by the wiles of the other; but it often happens that the entrapper afterwards rues the capture as much as—or even more than—the entrapped. So, it often happens that

Girls who are deliberately seeking husbands think love may be won by artifice. Not until well on in years do

Women know that, by men, love and artifice are considered mortal foes.

To win him a wife by artifice would be to a man a thing impossible and abhorrent: yet

To win her a husband by artifice is to a woman a thing quite natural. But

When (if ever) the man discovers that he was won by artifice, there are apt to be several bad quarters of an hour. For, when all is said and done,

The man, free and easy, thoughtless and untrammeled, knowing he may pick and choose, never chooses till—till—there comes the woman he thinks he wants. Then he says point blank he wants her. Should it ever be revealed to him that his Want was the result of her Artifice, a very different complexion is put upon that Want. On the other hand,

The woman, deprived of the power of choice, trammeled by convention, bound to wait till asked for, quite naturally resorts to artifice. And yet, curiously enough, and a thing incomprehensible by man,

A man whom a woman has won by sheer artifice, she can love to the end of her life. But, after all,

What a refuge, to man, is work—or play! Alas!

Women has no refuge. So,

Men cannot suffer long; women do.

A man flies to work, or sport, or to the gaming-table, or to drink. A woman. . .

He who can tell what a woman does in the sorrow of the soul, will tell us much.

Some women, in sorrow of soul, eat out their hearts in silence; other women, in sorrow of soul, will tell us much. Some women, in sorrow of soul, eat out their hearts in silence; other women, in sorrow of soul, eat out the hearts of others, not in silence. But

Take a taciturn woman seriously. For always

A taciturn woman has suffered much:

A taciturn woman is a lonely one. And probably,

It is only women who really know loneliness:

Give a man a full meal and an outlet for his energy—he is fairly contented; for

A man always has friends or a club; women rarely have either.

THE MOST SUPERB OF PHYSICAL charms are powerless unless fired by imagination; as the most destructive of explosives is harmless without a cap or a detonator. But,

Given, a detonator, and the coarsest powder can work tremendous havoc.

WHAT, PRECISELY, WILL BRING A particular man to her feet—that is, par excellence, the feminine problem: and many and various are the experiments by which she tries to resolve it. And,

Few are the men who learn that were won by experiment. For,

Man succumbs to his emotions. He cannot comprehend how it is that

Into feminine emotion, calculation often enters.

AS THERE ARE TWO CLASSES of warriors, so there are two classes of women:

There is the warrior who conquers the world from sheer love of conquest—an Alexander, a Genghis Khan, an Attila, a Napoleon; and there is the warrior who captures a kingdom for the sake of possession—such is your Norman William.

So, there is the woman whom no conquest contents—Aholibah, Cleopatra, Mesalina, Faustine; and there is the woman who is happy with a husband and home—Deborah, Vlmnia, Calpurnia mother of Gracchi.

One thing, from men, women cannot abide, and this is a hostile and Reasonable attitude. And naturally, since

It is only man's reason that is hostile to women. And When a man clothes himself with reason as with a garment, woman slinks away. And, quite naturally:

Reason and emotion are mortal foes; and

It is on the field of emotion that the battle of love must be fought. For,

In the battle of love, the woman chooses and entrenches her position; the man has to act on the offensive. But

Only emotion can cope with emotion; reason but beats the air. Wherefore,

A wise man will neither oppose nor appeal to a woman through reason.

Who can penetrate to the motives of a woman's coaxings? Yet Foolish is the man who questions the motives of a woman's coaxings. Yet

Not to be sure of a woman's coaxings—not upon this side Phlegethon is there a more poignant position.

In loving one woman a man believes in all women. And

Not till a woman is loved are her finger-tips objects of devoutest worship. On the other hand,

It cannot be said that in loving one man a woman believes in all men. Which little distinction is proof, perhaps, that

Love blinds the eyes of men, but opens the eyes of women. In other words,

Passion obfuscates man's prevision; it does not obfuscate a woman's.

Man gives the rein to passion or ere he knows whither it leads;

A woman gives the rein to passion only after she has found out whither it leads. But when the goal is known, perhaps

Women are more implacable votaries of the Implacable Goddess than are men. That is the say,

A woman keeps her head till she can give her heart, then she gives it utterly;

A man (perhaps because he has no heart) soon enough loses his head. So,

Before the gift, a woman's qualms exasperate the man;

After the gift, the man's indifference exasperates the woman;

IT IS FOLLY TO THINK that love and friendship exhaust the varieties of human relationships:—

The relationships between earthly souls are as complex and multiform as those between heavenly bodies.

In one thing does friendship excel love: it is always reciprocal; one friend presupposes another. Not so a lover.

Friendship is largely a masculine sentiment;—except among schoolgirls.

The friendship that exists between a man and a woman should be called by another name. It cannot be wholly Platonic; it need not be wholly Dantesque. Yet women generally strive to make it the one; and men often try to make it the other. And yet again,

How many women there be, would, if they could, transmute love into friendship! That is to say,

Women regard a man's friendship as a delicate flattery to themselves; yet they instinctively know, though they try hard to forget, that a man's friendship for a woman is extremely likely to transcend the bounds of friendship.

If only friendship would keep within bounds! How many women deceive themselves into thinking that were devoutly to be wished! Yet probably, as a matter of fact,

The very woman who avers she regrets that your friendship is not mere Platonic, would resent the Platonism did it exist. Possibly not every woman will understand this. Assuredly no woman will admit it. And yet,

It is impossible to conjecture in what an exchange of confidences may terminate: it may be a kiss, or it may be a quarrel. But

Confidences are evoked rather by friendship than by love:

A woman will tell a man friend what she will not tell a lover.

Few lovers will understand this, fewer still will believe it. Yet it is true, and the explication of its truth would be long and complex. This much may be said:

Love idealizes; friendship does not. At the same time,

Love probes the innermost recesses of the womanly nature; and, until the woman is wholly won,

The woman resents the inspection of love. She knows that,

To stimulate love, the woman must conceal, not reveal;

To stimulate love, the woman must conceal, not reveal. Furthermore,
Never was there a man who could be at once friend and lover.
Which is only one more proof that
Never will the sexes understand each other.
I use the word in its purely conventional sense.

THE MALE WAS EVER THE more susceptible sex. And for this reason,
Next to sympathy, flattery is perhaps woman's most effective weapon. And
No masculine shield there is which woman's flattery will not pierce. For
Man—man, alert in the hunt, keen in business, circumspect with his fellows, terrible in war, man is pristine and simple in matters emotional, and an easy prey to emotional wiles. In the long journey of evolution from Amoeba to Man,
The masculine sex has developed muscle and mind;
The feminine sex developed and perfected the emotions. Accordingly,
Man's emotions are the primitive weapons of a savage;
Woman's emotions are arms of precision. Yet
Sometimes woman deplores the unequal contest—perhaps deplores her too-easy victory. Since,
In domestic life, the weapons are laid aside, the pair are then—presumably—unarmed and defenseless. For, though,
A mat has to be won by weapons,
Marriage should be a treaty of peace: thenceforth the combatants are allies.
Many a man, when ensnared, has been amazed at the size of the meshes.
Only a woman knows by what open methods floundering men are captured.

HE WHO BY REASONING THINKS to find out woman, must either be a philosopher or a fool—probably both.
Less of a philosopher and more of a fool is he who thinks to extract from woman her reasons for her actions. The woman who can give reasons for an action is yet to be born. The reason is plain:
Women act upon intuition, not upon reason. And
He who could make a logical sorites out of feminine intuitions could make a philosophical system out of nautical almanacs. And yet, probably,

ARNOLD HAULTAIN

Could we only determine her orbit, a woman's intuitions are as exact as the paths of the planets. Unfortunately,

Such are the perturbations to which a woman's orbit is exposed that no masculine astronomy can construct its ephemeris. Alack, How many anxious star-gazers are there among men! The orbit of the ordinary male man it is not as difficult for a woman to compute, inasmuch as

The ordinary male man revolves unusually about two foci: his Appetites; and his Ambitions.—Which is the major and which the minor. . . However,

You may trust women to know when he is in peri-and when in aphelion.

Many a spouse has no difficulty in explaining away to her lord actions about the character of which even his initiate friends have no shadow of doubt. For

A woman's perception is preternatural. But no; it is natural enough, since

From the days of the first woman to the days of the New one, love, its wiles and its whims, has been the serious business of woman.

WOMEN KNOW MUCH BETTER THAN men that stolen bread is sweetest. In consequence,

Men steal almost everything they get from women.—At least they think they do. Which is the same thing.

IF THE SEXES WERE TO change places, more marriage licenses would be taken out.

'FRAILTY,' SAYS MAN, 'THY NAME is woman,'—and then he takes advantage of it.

AT ARM'S LENGTH IT IS difficult to offer a helping hand. Yet it is hazardous to reduce that distance.

NEGLECT IS THE UNPARDONABLE SIN in a woman's eyes. Woe to the man who is guilty of it.

IF A WOMAN POSSESSED ONLY a man's tact, what fallings-out there would be!

MAN'S *SUMMUM BONUM* IS TO combine a comfortable home with congenial club.

Woman's *summum bonum* is the almost equally incompatible combination of a well-regulated family and the height of fashionable gaiety.

Man's *infinum malum* is domestic distraction. Woman's *infinum malum* is social exile.

BETWEEN MAN AND MAN, TO lay another under pecuniary obligation is to jeopardize friendship. Between man and woman, a like cause brings about an opposite result.

THE MAN WITH SOMETHING OF the feminine about him often knows better than his more masculine rivals how to work upon feminine susceptibilities.

MOST WOMEN KNOW HOW MUCH to leave to a man's imagination.— But then, man has not much imagination. Besides,

Man's imagination is always highly complimentary to woman.

AFFINITY COVERETH A MULTITUDE OF sins.

TO ATTRACT SOMETIMES REQUIRES TEMPORARY repulsion. But

Some women miscalculate their satellite's orbit. With the result that either it rushes on to certain destruction, or it passes beyond the limits of gravitation.

The woman who to one man is no more than the sub-stratum of frock and bonnet, is to another man the centre of gravity of the created cosmos.

When she is such centre to more than one man, her horoscope is difficult to cast.

WHEN ONE HEART LAYS SIEGE to another , both sides throw up entrenchments; and this even when both belligerents are ready to negotiate for surrender. But,

Never, never show that you expect capitulation. And

Flank movements are not to be recommended.

IN CONVERSATION, THE LAST THING a woman expects from a man is information, unless it be information concerning himself. In fact,

Talk is a mere subterfuge. It is what is left unsaid that tells. Nevertheless,

When once the troth has been plighted, both *M* and *N* try to utter what has been left unsaid. But always with indifferent success. Alack and well-a-day,

Can Love ever say what it feels?

IT IS DIFFICULT TO SAY to which sex it is a greater compliment that widows always prove such successful fascinators. Either they still have a penchant for mankind, despite their intimate acquaintance with him—in which case the men may congratulate themselves; or else they have so completely found men out that they find no difficulty in entrapping them—in which case it is the women's turn to applaud.

WHEN OUR FEELINGS ARE UNWITTINGLY hurt by a beautiful woman, the pain is largely tempered by a subtle pleasure, which proceeds from a feeling that, inasmuch as we have been undeservedly pained, we merit her sympathy, perhaps even her affection.

WOMEN SEEK NOT SO MUCH man's esteem, as his admiration. In fact,

WOMEN WOULD RATHER ATTRACT THAN inspire.—Indeed, (by him who dared) it might be added that

Women would rather be kissed than be sonnetted,—which is mighty lucky for the majority of men!

THE MOST INTERESTING MAN OR woman is—well, perhaps the one most interested in us.

The least interesting man or woman is—well, perhaps the one most interested in him-or her-self.

NEVER FEAR BUT THAT ONE woman will urge your suit with another (unless, of course, that other is a rival); for

Match-making is one of the most fascinating of feminine avocations.

WHEN A WOMAN ALLOWS IT to be understood that she considers herself irresistible to the other sex, she draws upon herself the odium of her own. By the other sex, however, such a woman is very differently regarded. Indeed,

Men regard the avowed coquette not at all with malice, but with a very opposite feeling, of which perhaps amusement, admiration, and a certain amicable defiance are the chief ingredients.

IT IS ONLY MOUNTAINS THAT are volcanic or are snow-capped; the plains know nothing of extremes of frigidity or fire.

TO THE WOMAN WHOM HE has ceased to love, the man is sometimes unconsciously cruel.

Towards the man whom she has ceased to love, the woman commonly acts a part.

FOR A WOMAN TO HUMILIATE one man in the presence of another is an offence which neither of the men is likely to forget. Nor will the one man have a less unpleasant recollection of it than the other.

IT IS CURIOUS TO LISTEN to the explanations by one woman of the reasons of the attractiveness of another woman. Very apt is she to say that the other woman is too "free and easy", too liberal of her favors, too expansive of her sympathy, too exhibitive of her charms.—Ahem!

Women know women. And

Women know that women know men. And

Women know that men do not know women.—Ahem!—Men in this respect are somewhat different:

A man usually regards not ungenerously the qualities of his successful rival; a woman never. The former will candidly admit the possession of a more potent charm; the latter will trace it to the crudest of causes. In a word,

The unsuccessful man blames, not his rival, nor the women he loses, but himself.

The unsuccessful woman blames, never herself, but either the outrageous meretriciousness of her rival, or the blindness of the man she loses. From which it may once more be deduced that The unsuccessful woman blames, never herself, but either the outrageous meretricousness of her rival, or the blindness of the man she loses. From which it may once more be deduced that Men are won by more primitive means than are women. And, alas for men (alas also for many women),

The majority of men are so blind, so abominably blind, that they cannot distinguish the women who are really in love with them, from the women who pretend to be in love with them, but are not. For because,

So completely do women know men, that it is easy for any woman to delude any man. This is one of the reasons why

Every woman is the rival of every other woman:

This woman will be herself, her own true, simple, and virtuous self; will resort to no subterfuge, adopt no meretricious methods, scorn to rely upon tactics or strategy, be ever reserved, reluctant, shy;—yet fail.

This other woman will openly and blatantly, overtly and unconcernedly, assail the masculine heart with word and look and gesture—and win.—Ach! the purblindess of the masculine heart! how it exasperates even the woman!

THAT MAN HAS SUNK LOW who cannot recognize and respect the remnant of sex even in a degraded woman.

WOMAN CAN PERSUADE THEMSELVES—AND MEN—FAR more easily than can a man, of the propriety of their actions.

MAN IS POWERLESS BEFORE AN injured woman. He has no more dangerous foe than this.

IT IS THE MAN WHO seeks excuses. The woman braves it out.

COQUETRY IS LOVE'S LADY'S-MAID. She is accessory and ancillary to Love; she bedizens Love, she tricks her out in gay apparel.

When Love's lord and master enters, my lady's maid is dismissed. (It might be as well sometimes to recall her.) And

Nudity ousts coquetry.

CHASTITY IS A WORD WITH as many shades of meaning as there are peoples—perhaps as there are individuals—upon the face of this habitable world.

Women think chastity is a virtue primarily insisted upon and enforced by men. They mistake. 'T is a virtue primarily insisted upon and enforced by women: For

When that divine, unique thing Love comes to a woman, if she be not chaste, it is she who deplores the fact. The man may easily enough be deceived; her own heart a woman can never deceive. Besides,

With what righteous indignation women themselves visit unchastity!

Between the sexes, resentment is the worst of defensive weapons: in the hands of a man it is like a cow-hide shield opposed to Mauser bullets; in the hands of a woman, like a parasol on a cloudy day. Since

Woman penetrates resentment by ridicule; man treats it with dull indifference. And

A snub from a woman is never forgotten. And for two reasons: because

(a) The lord of creation hates to be floored by the jiu-jitsu of feminine raillery; and because

(b) The last thing a man expects from a "ministering angel" is mundane mockery. Besides,

Deliberate derision murders, not only affection, but admiration.

A blush needs no apologies. (Why? Because

Always a blush is spontaneous, uncontrollable; and

If there is any one thing a man likes to see, it is a spontaneous, an uncontrollable action in woman.)

When the man has declared himself hers and hers alone; has given proof of the truth of such declaration; has bound the woman to himself by terms dictated by herself then, but not till then, the woman acts spontaneously and without control; then she blushes. But

Seek not, impulsive masculine lover, to explore too many of the mysteries of this thy feminine helpmeet. Perchance she feels herself so much above thee that she blushes to give the herself. Perchance she regards thee so much a symbol of the god-like, that she blushes for because she is not more worthy. But far more probably she blushes for because she betrays to thee a mortal, a divine and cosmic secret. For

There is a divine and cosmic secret hidden beneath every blush.

Ah! man, man, peccant, impulsive, passionate man, little knowest thou of the divine and cosmic secret that underlies Love.

To thee, O man, it may be, 't is a momentary flash that irradiates the world, and reveals for a moment a sky above that world;

To thee, O woman, 't is the reverberating thunder that, echoing, rolls for ever after unceasing in thy ears. Is this why,

Between a man and a woman, a single look will sometimes change the complexion of an intimacy of a life-time? And

Not until that look comes—not until eyes look into eyes with a penetration supernatural—is acquaintanceship metamorphosed into love.

IT IS A FAVORITE FICTION amongst women that a rejected suitor either will not marry or marries the first girl he meets. Because,

To marry another woman after having offered inalienable and unalterable fidelity to one, would otherwise be a blow to "amour propere". And yet, strangely enough, or perhaps not so strangely,

This is a fiction but rarely maintained with regard to her own cardiac transportations. And for this reason:—

Woman is, and knows herself to be, a multiple personality;

Man, a tyro in emotions, is cast in a simpler mould. So,

A woman may donate herself piecemeal, or over and over again, yet deem herself perfectly loyal.—And perhaps naturally and legitimately; for,

That man who will comprehend and appreciate all the intricacies of feminine emotion. . . but there is no such being existent. Indeed even

Self-revelation is a task no daughter of Eve has achieved.

To SUM UP: BETWEEN MEN and women

The consummation of love is a bodily oblation, the outcome of spiritual obsession.—Must I explain this? No, I shall not. Suffice it to say that

The Heavenly Aphrodite is true friend to the Earthly. So

Nothing offends love; since love finds in all that savors of the mortal only a symbol and epitome of the supernatural. And

There is in Love a cosmic force and secret incomprehensible, incommunicable by man.

Is not, after all, Love the one supreme and significant fact of the cosmos: indelible, indecipherable: efflorescing in Man; emerging from the material; idealizing the carnal; pointing to an inscrutable, a spiritual goal? Can it be that

If we could explain Love, we should explain the cosmos? What if we could explain why it is that no one single isolated portion of the cosmos can live alone—and vaunt itself in itself sufficient—, but must seek some other single and isolated portion of the cosmos in order that that very cosmos shall continue, shall evolve, shall go towards its goal. . . Do we put our finger here upon some curious and recondite cosmic fact utterly transcending our mean comprehension?

Chapter X

On Jealousy

". . . la jalousie. . . monster odieux."

—Moliere

W are jealousy as you would 'ware wire: for it no psychiater has yet discovered a balm.

To make an experiment of jealousy is to make a very hazardous experiment indeed.

Jealousy is no proof of love, for
Often jealousy is but rancor under a sense of humiliation. Indeed,
Jealousy is a sign of weakness:
The lover whose self-confidence assures him of his pre-eminence fears no rival. Yet
Male self-confidence is peculiarly vulnerable where women be concerned, since,
As no man knows what it is appeals to a woman, he does not know on what to pride himself:
Even an Othello is jealous of even an Iago. Yet
It is only the spectators who see the folly of Othello. Desdemonas usually are helpless as they are oblivious.

The illicitly favored lover is never jealous of the husband; but of another illicitly favored lover, how jealous he is. But
Jealousy, like modesty, and like virtue, varies with every time and clime: what is customary in Cairo would rouse consternation in Kent, and what goes on in Vienna shocks New England. So,
How the husband favored lover differs also with every time and clime: here he is mulcted in damages, there he is shot down, in a third place he is tolerated.
How the woman thinks her husband should treat the illicitly favored lover—that you shall never find out.

The edacity of jealousy is unappeasable:

A wronged lover, in his pain, looks for more pain to bear: like a martyr in an ecstasy, he cries out for further tortures. In love one always sees higher unreachable heights; in jealousy always deeper unreachable depths. And

There is no wound but leaves its cicatrix.

Mistrust an unexpected change of front. So,

Does your erstwhile frowning lady smile? *cherchez l'homme*, or *la femme*. Since

To arouse jealousy in another feminine breast is sometimes the motive of feminine complaisance. Indeed,

Few women can forgo an opportunity of arousing jealousy, whether in a feminine or in a masculine breast.—Bethink thee of this little fact, O man, when next thy lady comports herself thee wards ultra-graciously.

To see the girl of thy heart—even if so be she not thine, nor not nearly thine—comport herself with another as she does with thee—ah! that gives a twinge to the masculine heart. Nay, lesser things than this will perturb this irascible organ: that the other should admire her charms—that she should accept such admiration. . . yet what cares she that these discomfort a man? For

A man's discomfiture is naught to a woman. In sooth,

Take a woman to task for her conduct, and with how soft an answer she will turn away your wrath, how deftly make light of your rival's advances!

Man, when he has won him a woman, is, in his great greed of possession, infinitely chagrined that he was not master of her past as of her present and future.—This goes by the name of *la jalousie retrospective*.

Women never know quite how to regard a man's jealousy. It flatters her, yet it pains her. She is the cause of it, yet she would believe it causeless. She deplores it, yet she would not have it quite away. It is proof of love, yet it is fatal to love. How to treat it, puzzles her. Implicit obedience to the man's wishes lowers her in her own eyes, and, consequently, so she thinks, in his. Yet so rabid is the emotion, she fears to provoke it too far. It places her in a quandary. She never knows what will evoke it; she never knows what course it will run: whether it will cement her lover's affections, or whether it will dissipate them forever.

It is love's most dangerous foe, and it is dangerous because it is insidious. If there is any one thing that puts a woman's wits to the test, it is a man's jealousy.

THE SHEEREST AND MOST INSENSATE folly a man can commit towards a woman is to let her know that another woman is cognizant of her jealousy of her. He may give the latter a very keen pleasure; but he gives the former a very keen pang. For

The cause of jealousy a woman may condone; the divulgence of her jealousy she will never forgive.

WHAT IRRITATES A JEALOUS MAN is the actions that cause his jealousy;

What irritates a jealous woman is the person who is the cause of her jealousy. In other words,

A jealous swain upbraids his mistress;

A jealous mistress objurgates her rival.

Chapter XI

On Kisses and Kissing

"Sag mir, wer einst das Kussen efrund?
Das war ein gluhend glucklicher Mund;
Er kusste und dachte Nichts daberi."

—Heine

Many are the varieties of kisses; as many, probably, as the varieties of kisses; as many, probably, as the variety of lips—and of the owners thereof. And

A kiss may mean so very much—or so very little. Wherefore

Look not upon the lips when they are red;—for although A kiss is a small thing, so is a spark. And always, though

A smile is an open window, a kiss is an open door.

Strange—strange—that from the momentary contact of lip with lip, an infinitesimal surface of epithelial tissue, there an be called up from the deeps of the soul emotions strange as deep; emotions vague and thrilling; emotions to the which to give utterance those lips are themselves all powerless. And

When to the conjoined lips there is added the bliss of an up-turned eye and embracing arms. . . Ah! well-a-day,

There are Edens for us still, if only we will eat not of the forbidden fruit.

The value of a kiss is determined by the personage on whom it is bestowed, not by the from whom it is besought: which, if it needs any explanation, means this, that

It is the man who ardently desires the kiss that puts the value upon that kiss, not the woman of whom it is desired. Yet women know that,

As with commodities, so with kissings, the greater the rarity, the greater the vale.

Osculatory transactions there be as lasting in their results as transient in their causes.

A CHEEK SURREPTITIOUSLY BRUSHED IN the dark is preferable to lips premittedly pressed by day.

WHAT AN EXTRAORDINARY MULTIPLICITY OF maneuvers a man will perform for "Just one kiss!" But

With the precise numerical equivalent of the expression "Just one kiss" algebra has not yet been found quite able to grapple. It is believed, however, to belong to Permutations and Combinations.

There is a very decided, but wholly indefinable, line of demarcation between the kissed and the unkissed woman. In other words,

The "status quo ante exosculationem" can never be re-established: hitherto the kisses may have been friends; henceforward they may be. . . they may be. . . But

Who shall say to what kissing may lead? Besides,

Much more kissing than is supposed goes by purchase than by favor. All which, probably, will be Greek to the uninitiated. Nevertheless, and at all times, and in all places,

A kiss is like faith: it is "the evidence of things not seen, the substance of things hoped for."

HOW APPALLING THE IMMENSITY OF the results due to the minutest of causes—a burning city from a lighted match; a life-long tragedy from a stolen kiss! In truth,

Fate is often another name for Folly.

A WOMAN WHO IS AFRAID of a kiss knows much. Amongst other things, perhaps, that

Kisses, like misfortunes, rarely come singly—and bear many things in their train.

DESPITE THE VARIETIES OF BEARDS and mustachios, never will you hear from your osculatrix the source of her knowledge of that variety.

If by any chance the divulgence leaks out—how the girl beshrews the mischance! For, though the man may hold his peace, she knows that she gives him to think.

IT TAKES TWO TO MAKE a quarrel. Yes: and it takes two to make the reconciliating kiss.

ARNOLD HAULTAIN

Chapter XII

On Engagements and on Being Engaged

Chalepon to mae philaesai
Chalepon de kai philaesai

—Anacreon

Perhaps the pleasantest and most satisfactory period in a girl's life is the time of her first youthful engagement:

Never is a girl more jubilant, never more buoyant, never so charming, so blithesome, or so debonair, as when she is the gazetted about-to-be bride of the man of her girlish choice. For

During her engagement, a girl is owned and petted; and Ownership and petting are dear to women—whether young or old:

Ownership is proof, at all events, that she is of value to the man—else the man would not sought to make her his; and

Petting is proof that the man properly appreciates the value. Yet meanwhile, anomalous as it may sound,

The engaged girl is still her own property, and is practically free. Besides,

What more delectable to a girl than to have captured and kept a real man? This flatters her, uplifts her, makes of her a woman at once: she holds her head higher she carries herself with an air; she shows off her capture. Besides, also,

The engaged girl is looked up to by her compeers, is congratulated y her elders. Even if she keeps the engagement secret, these compeers and congratulatresses do not (sometimes, alas! To her detriment).—In addition to all this,

What delight so unique as the preparation of the trousseau! Trousseau!—'T is a name of mystical import to man.

A woman's trousseau is symbol of two things—and perhaps dimly indicative of a third:

(i) it proves—what needs no proof—that, such is the unselfish nature of Love, never can it give enough, never enhance too much the gifts it gives. Accordingly the bride goes to the man appareled and bedecked to the best of her ability;

(ii) It is a subtle tribute to the sensibility of man, of the man in love, who is stimulated and pleased by dainty, it may be diaphanous, raiment. Lastly, since even that supernal thing Love is not unconcerned with matters practical,

(iii) It bespeaks as prophetic suspicion of the little fact that perhaps it is well to go to her husband's home abundantly provided with dainty raiment, inasmuch as the man not in love is not always so delicately sensible of their need.

A GIRL'S FIRST ENGAGEMENT IS peculiarly sweet: long does she remember, long meditatively dwell upon, its pettiest incidents. For, if any man dared give utterance to so outrageous an assumption,

The emoluments of a promise to marry are as sweet to the donatress as undoubtedly they are to the accepter.—And why not, pray? Nevertheless,

A certain practical sobriety supervenes upon subsequent affairs of the heart. For

The recurrence of love is apt to spoil its romance. And yet—and yet—

It is a question which woman after woman has put herself, in vain, whether 't would have been wiser to have accepted and retained the romantic love of unthinking youth, or to have waited for the more sober affection of the years of discretion.

Perhaps a girl hardly knows all that is meant by that thing called "love" or what is entailed upon her by that thing called an "engagement". She has played with love so much, that when a real and serious love is offered her, she still thinks it the toy that amused her. But

Soon enough does the man, if he is earnest—and a man never proposes unless he is in earnest—enlighten the girl of his choice: for

To a man, love never is a toy—though mere lust may be:

Men never play with love, as do girls: they play with lust,—as they play with bats and balls and fire-arms;

When men fall in love, they fall in love with a vengeance; and

The seriousness with which the man falls in love startles the girl.

The man demands so much; is so exacting' so peremptory; so unyielding; so frightfully selfish; so terribly jealous of the slightest look or smile or gesture bestowed upon any other than he, that the girl. . . well, the girl probably begins to think, either that the man is an unreasonable brute, or that her girlish notions of love were somewhat astray. Then one or two things happens: either the man goes off in a huff; or the girl mends her ways.

THE RECURRENCE OF A LOVE is a great shock to love. Love thinks itself a think unique, unalterable, supreme; a thing not made out of the flux and change of earthly affairs, but heaven-born and descended from the skies; that it should go and come seems to destroy the fundamental conception of love.

THE AFFIANCED MAN THINKS HE has won him the sweetest, the most sacrosanct thing that ever trode God's earth outside of Eden: a bundle of blisses, a compact little mass of exquisite mysteries, whose every tint and curve and motion are to him sources of wonderment and delight; he is at once humbled and exalted; he thanks high Heaven for the gift; for that comport himself worthy of such gift; for that this wondrous and mysterious little thing called "a woman" should of her own accord put herself in his arms, to be by him and by him alone cherished and nurtured till death them do part—this indeed gives the mail heart a very sobering, a very ennobling thrill; for beneath the heaving breast he so passionately loves, behind the eyes into the depths of which he so passionately looks, there stirs, he knows, that ineffable, that indefinable thing, a woman's heart; and that *to him* has been committed the keeping of that heart—this rouses in him the manly virtues as no other thing rouses them. Strong is the man who can live up to these emotions; sage the woman who knows what she has aroused.

THE PHILANDERER OR THE flirt—to whom love-making and love-taking have been a pasttime—is appalled at the seriousness of love when real love is offered him or her. For often enough
    The philanderer or the flirt thinks compliments and cajolery the food of love: in time they discover that love is a veritable sarcophagus!

MANY AN ACCEPTED LOVER (BOTH masculine and feminine) tries to make up for coldness of passion by warmness of affection: a subterfuge of dubious efficacy. For though
    Affection seeks affection, passion is only appeased by passion. Yet
    When one loves passionately, and the other languidly accepts, it is well perhaps for that other sometimes to be a little "unfaithful to the truth" and to simulate an unfelt ardor. But, always this is of questionable value, for
    Love abhors simulation of anything even of ardor.

If MUTUAL CONFIDENCE IS NOT established at the moment of betrothal, it will never afterwards be established. And

Woeful will be the plight of those between whom mutual confidence is not then established. For

Mutual confidence is the only atmosphere in which love can breathe.

An ENGAGED MAN, LIKE A hungry man, is an irascible man. And How often a fiancée is sore put to it, not only to satisfy him, but to pacify him!

A WOMAN WILL OFTEN BLANDLY ask why the two rivals to her hand should not be friends! Yet it is significant of much that she does her utmost to keep them apart! Indeed,

In no instance are a woman's tact and finesse so exercised as in playing off one man against another.—And yet usually she delights in the task; for

Being-made-love-to is to women what killing—whether of men or of animals—is to men. In a word,

To be sought after is to woman what war or the chase is to man.

The MOMENT A WOMAN ACCEPTS a man, then and there he becomes her lord and master. And this she unconsciously knows—nay, expects. If the man does not then and there exercise his lordship and show his mastery, he will find it difficult to do it later on. But of course

No woman will ever be got to admit that her newly-won man is her master. Nevertheless it is counsel that every man should lay to heart, for

Unless a woman is dominated (N.E. not dominated over), she tries to get the upper hand. And

Only two instances there are in which the woman should retain the upper hand: when the man is either a philosopher or a fool;

When a man is both (and the combination is not uncommon), she would be a fool if she did not retain the upper hand! But

Little does a woman esteem him to does not sway—nay, who does not sacrifice, it may be: her to his will.

Of THAT ENGAGED PAIR WHO can confidingly speak the one t the other of the dawn of their mutual attraction, little need be feared; if they cannot, very much may be feared. For

Love, without confidence, is as defunct as faith without works. For

ARNOLD HAULTAIN

If *M* cannot confide in *N*, it probably means that K and L have, or that O and P will.

So TREMENDOUS ARE THE RESULTS of the gift of self that Nature herself seems to have ordained that the feminine sacrifice shall be utter and complete. For,

A man's interests may be many and and behold, a bold girl will appear and carry off the shy man! Perhaps to the life-long chagrin and sorrow of all three.

Often, oh! how often, an awkward and sophisticated youth and a prim maid with down-cast eyes will sit together, waltz together, and the one never get one inch the nearer to the other, though soul and mind and body crave a closer union. The youth would give the solid earth—nay, the solid earth would be naught—to gain him the courage to clasp the maiden to his breast; yet, so intense his awe, he would not strain a spider's web to risk the maid's good will.—The maid—who shall say what passes in her mind? That the youth should adventure, she could wish; yet his very hesitancy bespeaks his devotion true. Were he to fall about her neck, embrace her close, and demand the kiss of love—most like she would recoil aghast—at first! Yet if he desisted—she would also recoil aghast.—What should he do, poor awkward youth? what she?—One thing onlookers will do: smile, and simper, and smile again; but in their inmost heart of hearts they will envy that awkward youth, that simple maid. For because, in this the first symptoms of unsolicited and reciprocal love, they will recognize something of the divine and mystical nature of Love itself, of Love untrammeled by convention or law; of Love itself, in its purity, its intensity, its diffidence, its terrifying yet restraining force.

Ah! Love, not in every conflict art thou victor crowned.

Chapter XIII

On Marriage and Married Life

ariston andri ktaema sympathaes gunae.

—Hippothoon

Marriage laws are framed, not for or by the likes and dislikes of men and women, but by the exigencies of social, often of political, economy. Therefore

Men and women's likes and dislikes are obliged to conform to the usages demanded by social and political economy: so

In Turkey women accept with a good grace the custom of a plurality of wives; in Tibet men accept with good grace a plurality of husbands. In the western world. . . Humph!

Always will there be everywhere prevalent a latent hostility between the likes and dislikes of men and women on one hand, and the laws enforced by a social and political community on the other. This is why

Always there will be those who will try to "reform" the marriage state: some looking only to the likes and dislikes of men and women, others only to the advantages which shall accrue to the State. So,

Some there will be will always advocate a loosening of the marriage bond, others who will seek to make it indissoluble. Both should remember that

The unit of the State is the family; therefore the State makes laws, not to suit the tastes or convenience of the husband and the wife, but for the good and preservation of the family. All of which, surely, is right and proper, since

It is the business of the State to make laws governing the welfare of the generations to come. In fine

The children—they are the pivot about which all matrimonial controversies should turn.

Reformers of marriage laws should seek a preventative, not a cure; since

It is doubtful whether the ills of matrimony are really curable, for, generally speaking,

Matrimonial incompatibility is a malignant, not a benignant, disease; its prognosis is doubtful; nor does it run a regular course.

MANY ARE THE WOMEN WHO, soon after marriage, silently turn over in their minds this little problem: whether it were better to marry the man they loved but who did not love them; or to marry the man who loved them but to whom they were indifferent. And

The man a woman ultimately marries will give her no clue to the solution. And for the following reasons:

(i) He, fond wight, does not know that any such problem is agitating her little brain; and

(ii) She, of course, dare not divulge the factors of the problem. In short,

Most marriages are brought about by the following simple, yet fateful, consideration: The man marries the woman he wants; the woman marries the man who wants her. The two propositions, though apparently identical, often produce results very far from identical. And yet,

Sometimes—sometimes—that glorious dream comes true, in which a hale and heart-whole youth implants the first pure passionate kiss upon the lips of a hale and heart-whole girl.—Ah, happy twain! For them the sun shines, the great earth spins, and constellations shed their selectest influence. 'T is a dream that all youth dreams. 'T is a dream makes wakeful life worth living.

Ah! the wild dream of youth! The maenad dream! The spring-time dream!

Of the maid: the dim, dim dream of stalwart man offering a love supreme without alloy, and taking, forceful, a love as flawless, as supreme; a steady breast on which to lean, strong circling arms, a face set firm against the world, a face that softens only to her up-turned eyes that seek the lover who is hers and hers alone; a dream of music, color, and the swaying dance; of rivals splendidly out-shone; of home and friends and trappings; of raiment. Retinue; of ordered bliss; and by and by, in a still dimmer far-off time, a time un-whispered to herself, of baby-fingers, baby lips. . .

Of the youthful man: a vivid dream, involved, unsteady, shifting; a dream of lust and love and smoke, and flame and fame; of cuirass and horse and saber; of blood and battle; of high place; of many dominated by his look and gesture; of mighty man, and orders issued, preemptory, not to be gain said; also of lithe arms, a supple waist, sweetly-soft entwining limbs, a gentle girlish woman all his own who never was another's and always will be his; and an heir and household gods.—Ah! the wild dream of youth!

Youths, dream ye while ye may! And you, ye aged, I charge ye do not wake them: it is the dream makes wakeful life worth living. And yet—and yet,

Sometimes—sometimes, alack and fie for shame, things come to such a pass, between husband and wife, that a modus vivendi has to be tacitly agreed upon. In that case, alas!

Too often, between husband and wife, it depends upon who is the better actor and liar—to their shame be it said. But before this happens, much else must have happened. For,

Here and there, ahem! we meet a woman who is like the moon: she circles sedately round, and dutifully faces, the planet to which she is united; but that planet does not know that she is irradiated and warmed by a far-distant sun—a sun which symbolizes, ahem! Duty, or Necessity, or Affection for her children, or (tell it not in Gath) Affection for another.

And here and there, ahem! we meet a man who, like the sun, shines steadfastly enough upon his own earth, but shines also, all unbeknown to earth, upon other earths—and errant comets—and small aerolites.

As it is usually physical or sentimental characteristics that bring a man and a woman into the field of mutual attraction, so it is generally physical or sentimental characteristics that drag them apart. Thus,

A clever wife will put up with a stupid husband, and an intellectual man will get on admirably with a dull but domestic woman. But

If either party to the marriage contract disregards or is unable to appease the demands made upon him or her for sympathy or emotion, there is likely to be trouble; for

Sentiment, not intellect, is the cementing material in marriage, and

If a man and wife cannot effuse a mutual sentiment, gradually they will grow apart. Indeed,

The demands of the emotions are at once more imperious and tyrannical, and more fastidious and critical, than are the demands of the mind. Of all of which, what is the moral? This:

The married pair who would live in amity, not to say in affection, must so live as that each shall persuade the other is the sole personage under the roof of heaven that he or she desires. Alas!

The unwritten motto of many a married couple is: The Heart Knoweth its own Bitterness.

ARNOLD HAULTAIN

MARRIAGE REVEALS THE MOODS OF a man.

What is an ideal marriage? That perhaps in which the man is to the woman at once friend, husband, and lover. But some people prefer these functions distinct.

That is a happy marriage in which a woman's husband is also her confidant. And always,

Husband and wife should move like binary stars: revolving about a common centre; mutually attractive; and, unless closely viewed, presenting a single impression.

MATRIMONY IS SOMETIMES A TERRIBLE iconoclast. Whether it throws down the images of false or of true gods, depends on the religion of the worshipper.

IT WOULD BE DIFFICULT, SOMETIMES, to determine whether constancy was an autogenous or enforced virtue.

NEVER PLAY PRANKS WITH YOUR wife, your horse, or your razor.

THERE IS A THING WHICH not gold nor favor nor even love can buy. Its true name is secret; but it is content to be called Sympathy. Accordingly,

Let no man or woman think when he or she has won wife or husband all has been won that is necessary. For,

If sympathy cannot be gained from one quarter, it will probably be sought in another.

AT THE MOMENT OF THE formation of a matrimonial syndicate of two, each member of this as yet unincorporated joint-stock company verily believes that each has put into the concern his whole real and personal property. Yet it is to be feared that, although

The woman, possibly, invests her whole capital, the man—often, no doubt, unwittingly to himself—retains not a few unmatured bonds and debentures. That is to say,

Love, it is to be feared, is often enough a bargain in which the woman comes off second-best. For

A woman gives herself; man accepts the gift.

Rarely, if ever, does a man give himself. He cannot. His work, his play, his politics, his friends, his club—these are matters to him highly important.

To a woman the only highly important things are: her husband and her home.

A WOMAN RULES UNTIL SHE tries to rule,—which will be an enigma to many.

OUT OF A WIFE'S OBEDIENCE will grow her governance; never out of her dominance.—Those who think this sheer nonsense, are welcome to think so. But it is worth thinking about.

A MAN OUGHT TO RULE his wife. Granted. But he cannot do this unless he rules himself. The Colonel of a Regiment cannot command if he himself breaks the King's or the State's Regulations. And

An uncontrolled wife deems her husband indifferent—or weak. The number of husbands who, though they think they rule, yet in reality are ruled, would astonish—not their wives, but themselves.

It is customary to call the man the head of the household; yet, between man and wife, it is a question after all whether it is not the stronger will and the cooler judgment that should, and generally does, guide the family, independent of sex or custom.

As IN THE SOLAR SPECTRUM, so in love: beyond and intermingled with the visible rays of passion are numerous actinic but invisible rays of affection, invisible to careless spectators, but known and felt by the recipients. These, too, must be introduced if the connubial domicile is to be warmed as well as illuminated.

THE MARRIAGE TIE LOOSENS ALL other ties. In fact,

Neither men or women are always aware of the absoluteness of the marriage tie: thenceforward the woman belongs not to her own people, hardly to herself.—As to the man, well,

Often a wife will actually be jealous of the time and attention her husband spends on things and matters unconnected with her—his work—his play—his politics—his friends—his club.

MANY ARE THERE WHO STILL believe that the marriage service, like a legal indenture, irrevocably entails the whole estate of a human heart. In sober truth,

There never was a married couple yet who had not to purchase their own happiness. And

The only charms that increase in value as time goes on are the charms of character; beside these, those of person, and even those of mind, are weak. In short,

In marriage, as in every human relationship, it is character that avails and prevails, naught else.

CHEMISTS DRAW A DISTINCTION BETWEEN a chemical and a mechanical mixture. Moralists might discover the same in marriage.

TO ENCIRCLE MONOGAMY WITH AN ever-increasing halo of romance—that is a problem deserving of study.

Monogamy is one of the disharmonies of life; it seems (as I have said) to be the decree of politics rather than of nature.

But surely polygamy or polyandry would be more disharmonious still.

MARRIAGE RENDERS NO ONE IMMUNE. That is to say;

Unless husband and wife both avoid infection, both can catch amatory fevers.

THE WOMAN WHO HAS LEARNED how to minister to a man's creature comforts has learned much. And

It has disconcerted many a young wife to discover how important a part of her education this is! Since

It is certainly sometimes hard to reconcile a suitor's poetic protestations with a spouse's prosaic requisitions.

IN THE GAME OF LIFE a man may venture many stakes; a woman's fate is determined by a single throw of the dice. Thus,

How often it happens that a young and inexperienced maid will look about her, will weigh and consider, will pick and choose, and, when she thinks she has found a man to her purpose, will set her cap at him will attract him, enslave him, bring him to her feet, make him propose, accept him as husband, give him all the sweets of engagement, regard herself and proclaim herself his affianced bride,—all with most prudential—it may be, most praise-worthy—motives. On a sudden, the man discovers that this was no real attachment, but a fictitious, almost an enforced, one; that the methods (so he thinks) were artificial, the results delusive. What happens? The man withdraws—politely—gallantly: t'was a mistake; he is sorry; they are unsuited; he did not know his own mind; he is sorry;—and so on, and so forth. They separate. And, in this concatenation of circumstances, action for breach of promise is out of the question.—Besides, often enough, the girl, through pride or through sheer chagrin at the indifference of the man, pretends acquiescence.—What happens to the man? Nothing. If his senses were stirred, he himself is heart-whole. He gave nothing; he merely received. He proposes again to somebody else; is accepted; marries happily; rears a family. What happens to the girl? Everything. The man gave her nothing; she gave all—her lips, her looks, the recesses of her heart; the premonitions of the gift of her self; for, when she leant on him, looked up to him, clung to him, felt his strong encircling arms, was perturbed by his ardor, she gave that which was not to give again. Such woman is to be pitied. For, however much she may strive to make it appear that she gave nothing, that she had all to give again, not even her own soul will bear her witness, and sooner, or later, a subsequent lover (and such girl accepts the first lover that offers) will find a void where he hoped to find an inexhaustible treasure. For the woman cannot forever keep up a fictitious affection; and languid looks, and eyes that will not brighten, and smiles which are so evidently forced, bespeak her sympathies elsewhere.—But, as Heine said, this is an old story often repeated. Wherefore

Let us pity women! The dice they throw are their hearts—and they have only one throw:—when they have thrown away their hearts—Pity women!

Men have so many dice to throw: income, status, title; virility, fortune, fame; good spirits, good connections, good looks; an air, a figure, a soul-stirring voice; manners, breeding, force; a good name, a good bank account. The pity o' it is that

The whole marriage question revolves about a single point:

The man wants him a woman,—a woman who shall be his and only his;

The woman wants her a head of a home. And here again, and once again, we see the difference between the sexes:—

The one thing that the man wants is: a mate;

The one thing that a woman wants is: a head and provider of a household.

The man's thoughts never go beyond the woman;

The woman's thoughts always and at once travel far beyond the man—to the children, the household, the home. This is great Nature's

ARNOLD HAULTAIN

inexorable law. But little knows the woman, and less knows the man, that the nubile girl is merely obeying great Nature's inexorable law.

What price woman pays for her high office! for in this implicit, unquestioning, and unconscious obedience to Nature she performs perhaps her highest function. On all accounts, therefore, let us

Pity women! They obey so faithfully great Nature's law, and Nature so often plays them false—so very false, and so very often. Besides,

The woman who gives her hand without her heart finds in time that she has made a sorry bargain—a sorrier bargain, perhaps, that the woman who gives her heart with out her hand. For,

Passionately as a man desires a woman, the passionately-desired woman will in time discover that, unless she gives her heart with her hand, her gift suffers depreciation. And

Unless a woman gives her heart, how can she give her aid? Surely,

Unless a man's armor is buckled on for the strife of life by feminine sympathy, the fight is apt to be a sorry one at best; since

A woman's true business is to back her husband: if She leaves him in the lurch, there is little hope for him. For of a truth

The strongest man is handicapped in the struggle for existence unless he knows and feels that his wife is at his side—not pushing him so much as leaning upon him.

To simulate passion for an hour is possible; to simulate a life-long love—that is hard. For

Love is a thing unique and unalterable (in spite of its various alloys); clip the coin, and it will not pass current. For

Ideal matrimony is founded on a mono-metallic basis: no amount of silver will be accepted for gold. And yet,

How often M loves and N accepts the love! Poor M! Also (in the long run), poor N!

That, indeed, is a happy marriage where M gives and wants just what N wants and gives: where M and N just *want each other*. For

Give and take is the rule of a community of two, as it is of a community of ten thousand;

The ideal (and probably impossible) industrial community is that in which demand and supply are in exact equipoise. The same holds good in matrimony.

In wedlock, a virtuous, has probably less force than a vicious, example. That is to say,

A frivolous spouse is more apt to drag the couple down than is a serious spouse apt to lead the couple up. And

Many a mate there is (both masculine and feminine) feels like a pack-mule treading a precipitous pass.

Of every Audrey her Touchstone should be able proudly to say, "A poor. . . Thing, Sir, but mine own". In other words,

The homely violet deserves as tender cherishing as the rare exotic.

What portion of himself or herself any one complicated physical and psychological human being really and truly 'conveys' to another by means of the simple contract known as the "plighted troth" or that of a larger deed called the called the "solemnization of matrimony", is a riddle difficult of solution; and as to how much one may claim on the strength of one or other of these indentures, that is a more difficult problem still.

In no amatorial contract, probably, is it possible to include or to enumerate all the hereditaments, messuages, or appurtenances, involved. Certainly

How great so ever the community of interest, M and N remain for ever M and N.

Is there not always something in the "eternal feminine" which cannot quite coalesce with the ephemeral masculine? Probably,

Trust your wife with your purse, and seven times out of ten it will grow heavy.

Many a woman, by man, is accepted at her face value.

Many a man, by woman, is taken on trust. It is difficult to tell whether

More bad debts are contracted by giving credit than by taking at face value. For

The promissory note of marriage is undated and unendorsed. But

Children act as collateral security.

How often a girl, even an affianced girl, accustomed to a multiplicity of admirers, forgets the man of her ultimate choice she must then and there set above all other claimants!

If the man the woman chooses for husband does not stand in her estimation absolutely first and all other claimants nowhere there is bound sooner or later to be trouble. For

No man will play second fiddle to any body or any thing; and

The realm amatory is a monarchial, not a republican, one. In all realms, there must be a ruler, whether elected or hereditary.

Always a divided sway results in schism, whether in the family or in the state. And although

Often enough the wife proves herself the more effective Sovereign, the forms of monarchy must be conceded to the man, even though the executive is left to the woman.

How often the only breast to which one can go on to "rain out the heavy mist of tears" is the one inhibited!

Two wills are not so easily blended into one as that the task may be left to Cupid. Yet,

Unless Cupid has a hand in blending two wills, it is bound to be a sorry business at best.

Always and in all wedlock there comes a time when will conflicts with will.

If both wills are inflexible, one must break—or both will fly apart. But

Love and tact will relieve many a strain. Though sometimes one discovers that

Human eyes have a certain store of tears. It is not difficult to weep them all away. However,

In the final rupture between man and wife, it is the children that turn the scales. But, O ye young husbands and wives, remember that

Youth regards the whole world as its friend; age finds itself desolate in the midst of friends. Wherefore,

O youth, cleave unto the wife of thy bosom; since

A loving wife is worth a multitude of friends.

Sweet are friends, and fame is sweet; but sweeter far a wifely heart whereon to lay a weary head. But

Each married pair must solve its own difficulties as best it can. If any advice were worth the offering, it would be this:

O ye Husbands, and O ye Wives, if not for your own sakes then for your children's, lead a straight, clean, honorable life; any other sort of life leads to despicability, to dismalness, to disaster.—Which only means, after all, that

In the marriage relation, as in every relation—the social, the industrial, the commercial, the political—it is conduct, it is character, that counts, nothing else;

Beauty—Wealth—Culture—Grace—Wit—Intellect—Sprightliness—Vivacity—Humor—these are much but they are simply naught, and less than naught, when just this simple, single, yet insatiable thing called Man wants to live amicably, affectionately, martially, with that simple, single, but incomprehensible thing called Woman.

Character—Conduct—rule the world, the Matrimonial equally with the Municipal.

Chapter XIV

ON THIS HUMAN HEART

"The heart is deceitful above all things and desperately wicked; who can know it?"

—HOLY WRIT

I t does not take much to make two hearts beat faster than one.

THE HEART CAN DECEIVE ITSELF when it cannot deceive another.— Which will be cold comfort to some lovers, though it may console others.

TO ADMIT A SACRED VISITANT into the inner recesses of the human heart, those recesses must be neat indeed. Remember, too, that you can
   Never expect an angel to act as a charwoman; the sweeping must be done by the owner. Lastly,
   Unless each heart is permitted access to the other, their union is fictitious, perhaps perilous.—Explain these tropes who can.

NO MAN CAN TELL TO whom a woman's heart belongs; not even the man who calls the woman "his". And
   Let no man imagine that when he has won him a woman, he has won him a woman's heart. Since,
   Sometimes a woman will give her heart to one man and her troth to another. Besides,
   Many a heart is hard to read—especially if it is a palimpsest. Indeed, many are illegible to their owners. Nevertheless, That the woman should not know her own heart (as so often happens) terrifies the woman as much as it exasperates the man. Yet,
   That must be a curious love that causes the heart to hesitate. And yet,
   Many a man has debated for months whether to propose or not; and sometimes a woman will accept on a Friday the man that she refused point-blank of a Tuesday. But perhaps,

Where the heart hesitates, it is not so much a case of love as a case of convenience. For,

An overwhelming love leaves the heart of either doubt or debate. But alas,

The human heart seems to be an anatomical engine of such intricate and delicate mechanism that its workings are uncontrollable even by its owner.

Is a constant heart as hard a thing to manufacture in the world of life as is an immobile thing in the world of matter? And matter, so they say, is immobile only at absolute zero—when bereft of even molecular motion: a thing impossible to produce, and which to produce would require incalculable pressure and almost incalculable cold.

(Is there no chemical formula for "fixing" the impression of the heart?)

Who really held Burns his heart in thrall, Nelly Fitzpatrick or Mary Campbell or Ellison Begbie or Margaret Chalmers or Charlotte Hamilton or Jenny Cruikshank or Anne Park or Jean Armour or Mrs. Whelpdale or Mrs. Agnes McLehose? and who the heart of Goethe,—Gretchen or Kitty Shonkopf or Frederica Brion or Charlotte Buff or Lily Shönemann or the Countess Augusta or Charlotte van Stein or Bettina Brentano or Mariana von Willemer—or his wife, Christina Vulpius?

However, whether it is a provision of Nature, or whether it is due to the perversity of Man, probably the feminine heart is far more constant than the masculine, and perhaps any one of Goethe's or of Burns his inamoratas would have clung to him had he been faithful to her. And yet,

Would you have had Shelley stick to Harriet Westbrooke? and how shall one interpret his feelings for Amelia Viviani? What would have happened if Keats had lived and married Fanny Brawne—she who flirted with somebody else while he was sick and did not even know that he was a poet? Yet she was an inspiration to Keats, as Mary Godwin (and Amelia Viviani) were to Shelley. Ought Byron to have said 'No' to Claire or Lady Caroline Lamb or the Countess Guiccioli or any one of the many maids and matrons that besieged his heart? Could anything have kept Rosina Wheeler and Bulwer Lytton side by side,—Rosina Wheeler to whom, before marriage, Lytton could find write, "Oh, my dear Rose! Where shall I find words to express my love for you?" and to whom, after marriage, he wrote, "Madam, The more I consider your conduct and your letter, the more unwarrantable they appear"?

ARNOLD HAULTAIN

God in heaven! what a pitiful game it all is! And alas! as George Sand says, "All this, you see, is a game that we are playing, but our heart and life are the stakes, and that has an aspect which is not always pleasing."

MANY A MAN'S HEART HAS been treated as a football. Yes; but many a woman's heart has been treated as a shuttlecock.

HUMAN BEINGS THERE ARE—BOTH men and women—out of whom, at a mere touch, virtue seems to go: converse with them is stimulating; contact enthralling. And yet,

Powerful as physical or as mental attraction may be, permanently to retain the attracted object requires a profounder force. Perhaps, though,

Beauty and grace and brilliancy may attract; it is only something far more deep-seated that retains. In other words,

Charm of body and mind may appeal to body and mind; only the heart appeals to the heart. Those who know not this, and they are

Many, permit the heart to leak through the senses; with the result that, when demands are made upon the heart, that cistern is found to have run dry. So,

To philanderers and to flirts, when a great and true love comes, they do not comprehend it, and they cannot appreciate it. Wherefore,

Would-be lover, keep thy heart intact until it be required of thee.

YOU NEED NOT IMAGINE THAT, because you have once been permitted to see some way down into a human heart, that you will necessarily ever again be so permitted.

HARD WORDS BREAK NO BONES. But they often break hearts.

DRINK IS TOO OFTEN THE refuge of the masculine, and a rich husband the refuge of the feminine, broken heart.

EXTREME YOUTH THINKS THE WORLD is a toyshop—where anything may be had for the asking; old age regards it as a museum—where nothing may be touched.

NO HEART, UNDER REPEATED TEMPERINGS, can remain forever keen. And

As a little body sometimes has a very big pain; so an aching heart wonders that it can bear so much. And

What takes place in the quiet deeps of a troubled heart, who shall know?

THE WAY TO THE HEART is not through the head:

Between heart and heart, there are many channels. But three are in universal use: the eyes, the lips, and the finger-tips. Now the greatest of these is the eyes.

THE MASCULINE HEART WILL NEVER wholly understand the feminine, nor the feminine the masculine. (O the pity o' it!) And yet, after all,

The human heart is much more the same, whether it beats under a cuirass or under a corset.

Between the masculine heart and the feminine, perfect frankness is perhaps of questionable import. But why? It is difficult to say. Perhaps because

The aspirations and desires of the human heart are infinite and unappeasable. To attempt to formulate them is to frustrate them. For

It is as impossible for any two human hearts, as it is impossible for any two material things, to occupy the same space. Especially when we remember that

Between the masculine heart and the feminine is a great gulf fixed. Nay, rather

From youth to age, each human heart seems unwittingly to build about itself a high and ever higher-growing wall, impenetrable, indelapidable, not to be scaled by the look or speech or gesture. Never can heart coalesce with heart. And yet

The absolute and intimate coalescence of heart with heart—is not this, after all, the consummation that every lover seeks? To attempt that consummation by mere speech, it is this that is of questionable import. Since

Between heart and heart, speech is the paltriest of channels.

What a thin—yet what an invisible and impenetrable—film separates those two worlds: the one, that of the visible, audible, and tangible, the world of chatter and laughter, of convention, often of make-believe; and the other, the world of deep and voiceless emotions, of the feelings which know not how to give themselves utterance, of affections which crave so much and are so impotent to say or to seek what they crave!

It is like a layer of ice separating the hidden and soundless deeps from the aerial world of noise and motion.—What would not one heart give to break the icy crust and see and know what was really passing in another?—And how often we drown if we do break through!

The isolation of the individual human heart is complete. It is the most pathetic past in the universe, and it is that against which the individual human heart rebels most.

There must be some profound and cosmic problem underlying this fact which no philosophy—and no religion—can solve. That it is pathetic seems to prove it temporary, earthly, a matter of time and space; but, when will the individual human heart coalesce with the Heart of the Universe—which, perhaps, is the goal of all Life? For

It may be that these little terrestrial human individuals which we call men and women are after all only tiny and temporary centers of conscious activity in an ocean of infinite consciousness; as atoms are but tiny and temporary centers of energy in an ocean of infinite ether. Could we see the sum total of Supreme and Infinite Consciousness at a glance, perhaps individual men and women would dissolve into a mighty unity, could see and comprehend the whole of the luminiferous ether. Well, perhaps

Love is the only known means by which the individual heart can make any expansion whatsoever beyond its own bounds. Yet, alas! Nothing seems to break down the barriers of sense. The human heart beats its ineffectual wings in vain against the walls of its fleshly tabernacle. Will nothing unite the Boy and the Girl? Will nothing bring the Man and the Woman really together? Yet the Boy thinks that, were the Girl wholly his, he and she would be happy; and the Man thinks that, were the Woman and he to share every thought and every emotion, he and she would want naught else. Is the amalgamation impossible? Is the coalescence of thought and feeling outside the bounds of human possibility? What, then, impels mankind to crave it, to attempt it, to sacrifice so much for it?—There is a cosmic puzzle here with which nor philosophy nor psychology nor religion has yet attempted to grapple.

After all, pitiful as it may be, lamentable as it may be, it is true, and it must be said, that this human heart of ours goes through life hungry, very hungry and unappeased. For what it hungers, what it has missed, whereto it looks for sustenance, it itself does not know. Thus,

This feminine heart sighs without ceasing for because that other masculine heart upon which it staked all its all, and an all that meant so much, proved callous and indifferent;

That masculine heart ceases not to curse itself for resorting to such hasty and violent methods by which to obtain for itself an ephemeral and passing pleasure;

This feminine heart eats out its life with remorse for because it gave itself so unthinkingly when asked; though of a survey it thought that asking was a thing prompted by impulses as noble as they seemed divine; and

That masculine heart, when the tidal wave of heated passion has subsided, wonders how it was led captive by lures so deceptive and untried.

M regrets, and regrets in vain, that he did not await a purer and more permanent passion; and

N chews for a life-time the cud of persistent remorse for an hour's poignant pleasure.

Ach! this human heart knows nothing of itself nor anything of its fellow beating hearts. If it follows its bent, it is cracked; if it holds itself in leash, it aches. If it calls reason to aid, its soaring hopes are dashed, its romance spoiled, and it itself reduced to the level of a machine that calculates. If it acts on impulse and, meeting a heart that beats, so it thinks, in unison, unites itself with it, often enough that other soon palpitates to a different rhythm, or itself cannot keep time, and all things go awry.

Poor aching, beating, human heart! It cannot reason; it cannot count the cost. To it seems that impulse, divine and mighty impulse, is the sole law of the earth; in time it learns that impulse, the mightiest, the divinest, though it may be law in heaven, is sometimes a veritable nemesis on earth: it gives freely, gladly, without compunction; it finds the gift rewarded by consequences too pitiful for tears.

Alas, this human heart! Can no one advise it Is there no advice will help it? Must it always go wrong, and always suffer?—Well,—If one loves, one dare not reason; if one reasons, it is difficult to love.

THERE SEEMS TO BE SOMETHING cosmic, something transcending the bounds of the visible and tangible universe, in the desires and cravings of this same human heart; this little human heart beating blindly beneath a waistcoat or a blouse. Its owner is little bigger than a beetle or an ant, and the habitat of that owner is a speck in space; a pygmy in comparison with Sirius or Arcturus, and invisible from the ultra-telescopic confines of vision.

What it makes the desires and cravings of this human heart more important, more importunate, to its owner than the measuring of the vastest space? Why is it that the longings, the hopes, the disappointments, the desperate aspirations, and the passionate loves of little human hearts should cause to their possessors such prepotent commotions, such poignant qualms? Rigel and Betelgeuse and Algol rush through space, and about them probably circle numerous planets inhabited by countless and curious beings, each and all, perhaps, possessing hearts as perturbable as our own. And yet, if our own little earthly Jack cannot get our own little earthly Jill, what cares Jack what happens to Vega or Capella or to the great nebula in Orion? Jack wants Jill; and that want is to Jack the only thing in the sidereal heavens that matters.

The curious and perhaps semi-comical but wholly-pathetic thing about the whole matter is this: that though undoubtedly our little planet is part of and has a place in this great sidereal universe, and consequently all our Jacks and Jills are related to all the Jacks and Jills everywhere else, yet each little human heart behaves as it were the only heart in the sum-total of created things: if it enjoys, it calls upon all that is, to congratulate it; if it suffers, it cries aloud to high heaven to avenge its wrongs: it comports itself as if it and it alone were the only sensitive things in existence.—That is curious. That it wrongs may have been wrought by itself; that its fate may have been determined in the reign of Chaos and Old Night, or ere even cosmic nebulae were born, it does not dream: if Jill is indifferent or Jack morose,—either is enough to cause Jack or Jill to curse God and die. Is there some archetypal and arcanal secret in this the extreme, the supernal egoism of the human heart?

Of all of which, what is the moral?—Humph! Frankly, I do not know what is the moral. Only this I see: that each little heart creates its own little universe: the bee's, the that of its hive and the fields; man's, that of his earth and the stars. What may be above or beyond the stars, man no more knows than the bee knows what is beyond the fields. The heart—be it man's or a bee's—is the centre of its self-made sphere. Some day, perhaps, man's sphere will extend as far beyond the stars as today it extends beyond the fields. Then—who knows?—perhaps unlimited senses and an uncircumcised intellect may find themselves commensurate with this high-aspiring heart, and an emancipated and ecstatic Jack unite with a congenial Jill.

That there is a Universe, is apparent; that it is one and complete, we suppose; that there are in it Jacks and Jills, is indubitable; that these Jacks and Jills crave mutual support, sympathy, love, friendship, wifehood, sistership, companionship, brotherhood, is also indubitable.

If therefore the whole scheme of the Universe is not a farce, what does this craving of Love for Lover mean? And yet,

It is quite impossible to conceive of a Universe of Love, in which all the claims of Heart and Soul and Senses shall be eternally and infinitely satisfied? Nevertheless, on this little earth, perhaps

Ill betides the heart that leans overmuch on another. For, alas! Not even the entire immolation of one heart for another will satisfy that other.—Indeed, indeed,

In this life, would one seek comfort and solace, one must seek it—in one's own self, or in one's God. For

Only one of two things can comfort: To put the world under one's feet; or, to keep a God over one's head: only

He who is "captain of his soul", or he who commits his soul to God, can rise above fate.

There is a vacuum in every human heart. And the human heart abhors it as much as nature.

What will fill this cardiac void no mortal to this moment has found out. Art cries, "Beauty", and tries to depict it; Philosophy cries, "Truth, and strives to define it; Religion cries, "Good", and does its best to embody it; and numberless lesser voices in the wilderness cry, "Power", or "Gold", or "Work",—which is a narcotic, or "Excitement",—which is an intoxicant; and a many-toned changeful siren with sweetly-saddening music cries, "Love". And one pursues a phantom, and another clasps a shadow, and a third cloaks his eyes with a transparent veil, or steeps his senses in floods that will not drown.—No, what the human heart wants it does not know. And, what is more,

Pathetic problem amongst problems pathetic, often it puzzles this human heart to distinguish between the things which it is right and proper to seek wherewith to fill that void, and the things which are wrong and improper. Furthermore:

How apt is the heart to seek in the illegitimate for the satisfaction which the legitimate fails to give!—Problems ancient as Eden.

What does it want, this human heart, what does it so earnestly desire, so strenuously seek? All about it and about are beauty, friendship, mirth, and gladness; the sea and the earth and the sky; color and music and song; and to each, if he wills it, wife, or husband, and children and home.—Wanting is—what?—Ah!

One lesson this human heart has to learn, so easy to put into words, so difficult to carry out by deed; is this:

ARNOLD HAULTAIN

To get, the human heart must give.

The heart eats out itself; causes its own emptiness; creates its own void.

The selfish and egoistical life breeds always the vapid and vacuous heart.

Would you appease your own hunger? Feed the hungry hearts around you.

Do you crave fullness of joy? Give joy to the joyless.

Would you fill your own cavity, satisfy your craving, attain your desire, find what you seek? Give—give—give. The more the better, for

The greater the donation, the greater the repletion.

Nature gives, gives lavishly, wantonly, unquestioningly.

Every atom of soil, every drop of sap, goes to produce flowers and fruit and seed: root and branch and leaf are but carefully constructed means by which to transmute sunshine and soil and flower and fruit and seed. No tree lives for itself.

Shall, then, this human heart live for itself; gather and store up for its own delectation, for its own good?

There is no such thing as one's own good:

Goodness is mutual, is communal; is only guided by giving and receiving. Wherefore

O frail, weak, human heart, seek thou out carefully constructed means by which to transmute sunshine and soil and showers into flowers and fruit.

A Note About the Author

Arnold Haultain (1857–1941) was a British writer who produced a diverse catalog of books and essays covering sports, romance and war. Although born in India, Haultain spent his formative years in England and later, Canada where he attended the University of Toronto. Over the course of his career, he wrote more than 30 books including *The Mystery of Golf* (1908) followed by *Hints for Lovers* (1909). Haultain's work was also featured in multiple magazines across North America and Europe.

A Note from the Publisher

Spanning many genres, from non-fiction essays to literature classics to children's books and lyric poetry, Mint Edition books showcase the master works of our time in a modern new package. The text is freshly typeset, is clean and easy to read, and features a new note about the author in each volume. Many books also include exclusive new introductory material. Every book boasts a striking new cover, which makes it as appropriate for collecting as it is for gift giving. Mint Edition books are only printed when a reader orders them, so natural resources are not wasted. We're proud that our books are never manufactured in excess and exist only in the exact quantity they need to be read and enjoyed.

Discover more of your favorite classics with Bookfinity™.

- Track your reading with custom book lists.
- Get great book recommendations for your personalized Reader Type.
- Add reviews for your favorite books.
- AND MUCH MORE!

Visit **bookfinity.com** and take the fun Reader Type quiz to get started.

Enjoy our classic and modern companion pairings!

Printed in the USA
CPSIA information can be obtained
at www.ICGtesting.com
JSHW080002150824
68134JS00021B/2240

9 781513 266541